CULTURE SMART!
BANGLADESH

Urmi Rahman

·K·U·P·E·R·A·R·D·

ISBN 978 1 85733 695 5
This book is also available as an e-book: eISBN 978 1 85733 696 2

British Library Cataloguing in Publication Data
A CIP catalogue entry for this book is available from the British Library

First published in Great Britain
by Kuperard, an imprint of Bravo Ltd
59 Hutton Grove, London N12 8DS
Tel: +44 (0) 20 8446 2440   Fax: +44 (0) 20 8446 2441
www.culturesmart.co.uk
Inquiries: sales@kuperard.co.uk

Distributed in the United States and Canada
by Random House Distribution Services
1745 Broadway, New York, NY 10019
Tel: +1 (212) 572-2844   Fax: +1 (212) 572-4961
Inquiries: csorders@randomhouse.com

Series Editor Geoffrey Chesler
Design Bobby Birchall

Printed in Malaysia

About the Author

URMI RAHMAN is a Bangladeshi journalist and author with a Master's degree from Chittagong University. After working for several years on various newspapers and magazines in Bangladesh, she was awarded a UNESCO Fellowship to Michigan State University and to the Press Foundation of Asia in Manila, Philippines. In 1985 she joined the Bengali Section of the BBC World Service in London as a producer and broadcaster, and remained with them for eight years before leaving to work in local government in London. Urmi has published a number of books, both fiction and non-fiction, and has translated several books from English to Bengali. She now lives in Kolkata with her Indian husband, and regularly contributes to newspapers and journals in both Kolkata and Dhaka.

contents

contents

Map of Bangladesh

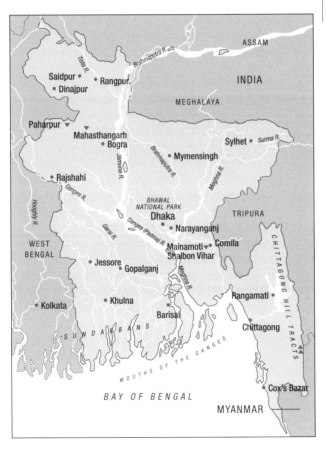

introduction

Bangladesh is a lush, green, fertile land situated on the Ganges Delta, adjacent to the Indian states of West Bengal, Assam, Meghalaya, and Tripura. With mountains and hilly areas in the northeast, this densely populated country is mostly flat, and criss-crossed by many rivers. Much of its coastline forms part of the world's largest mangrove forests, the Sundarbans, home to the Royal Bengal tiger and many other flora and fauna. Cox's Bazar in the southeast has the world's longest unbroken sandy beach. The cities are hot and crowded, but if you grow tired of the hustle and bustle it's easy to get to these places for a relaxing holiday, or to visit the country's ancient temples and shrines.

Bangladesh is a young country with an ancient history. The province of Bengal was divided when India became independent in 1947, and its mainly Muslim eastern part became East Pakistan. This was followed by years of upheaval, and in 1971, after a freedom struggle and a war, the east Bengali people finally gained independence as the People's Republic of Bangladesh.

Most Bangladeshis live in rural areas, and the majority are Muslim. Historically they have coexisted in harmony with many other faiths, and the Islam of Bangladesh is tolerant and inclusive compared to many Muslim countries of the world.

Bengali, or *Bangla*, is the lingua franca, and there are dozens of regional dialects. The Bengal delta region, once the hub of the southern Silk Route, has a long and rich cultural tradition. Over the centuries it has been influenced by Hinduism, Jainism, Buddhism, Islam, and Christianity. It is a land of writers, saints, scholars, and artists, famous for its music, dance, and drama; arts and crafts; folklore; literature; philosophy and religion; festivals and celebrations; and its distinctive culinary tradition. Life in both urban and rural areas is a mix of the modern and the traditional.

Bangladesh has been regularly hit by floods and cyclones, but, despite natural disasters and poverty, there is positive economic growth, and the country is one of southeast Asia's largest exporters of garments to Western markets.

The Bangladeshis are easygoing, relaxed, and amazingly resilient. They seem able to cope with any disaster, natural, man-made, or political. Whenever there is a crisis, they put aside their political divisions and come together to deal with it. Despite the daily hardships that ordinary people endure, they are friendly, warm, and hospitable.

When you first arrive in Bangladesh you may be overwhelmed by the crowds, the traffic jams, the humidity, and the lack of familiar facilities. Your perspective will change as you come to know its people. This book will introduce you to their culture and to the generous, creative, and genuine people beyond the headlines. To smooth your path it offers advice on what to expect and how to behave in different social situations, whether you are a tourist or you are traveling on business.

Welcome to Bangladesh! *Bangladeshe swagato!*

culture smart! bangladesh

Key Facts

Official Name	People's Republic of Bangladesh	Bangladesh became a sovereign country in 1971.
Capital	Dhaka	Population approx. 7 million. There is a constant flow of migration from villages and other areas to Dhaka.
Main Cities	The second-largest city is Chittagong. Other major cities are Khulna, Rajshahi, Sylhet.	Chittagong has mountains, rivers, and the sea, and the main seaport. The other seaport is Khulna.
Population	163,654,860 (July 2013)	Population growth 1.59% (2013 est.)
Ethnic Makeup	Bengali 98%, other 2% (includes tribal groups, non-Bengali Muslims) (1998)	There are a number of ethnic minorities, which can be found in Rangamati, Bandarban, Khagrachari, Cox's Bazar, Rangpur, Mymensingh, and Sylhet.
Area	55,598 square miles (143,998 sq. km)	
Climate	Tropical and quite varied. Mild winter; hot, humid summer; humid, warm rainy monsoon; and pleasant fall and spring.	There are six seasons: summer, monsoon, fall, hemanta (between fall and winter), winter and spring.
Language	The main language is Bengali (Bangla). English is widely used.	Different dialects in districts. The indigenous peoples have their own languages.

Religion	Islam is the state religion. The free practice of religion is guaranteed by the Constitution.	Muslim 89.5%, Hindu 9.6%, other 0.9% including Christian, Buddhist, Bahai, etc. (2004)
Government	People's Republic. Parliamentary system of government.	The prime minister is the head of state. The president is the constitutional head. Parliament has a 5-year term.
Business Hours	Government offices are open 5 days a week, 9:00 a.m. – 4:00 p.m. Private sector open 6 days a week, 9:00 a.m. – 5:00 p.m.	The weekly holiday is Friday and Saturday.
Currency	Bangladeshi Taka (US $1 = 78 Taka)	US Dollar/Pound Sterling are accepted.
Media	Media outlets, both print and TV stations have mushroomed. The press is largely free, though there are some controls. Major Bengali dailies: *Prothom Alo, Kaler Kantha, Janakantha, Jugantor, Shomakal, Shongbad, Ittefaq, Amar Desh*. English dailies: *Daily Star, The Independent, New Age, Daily Sun, Bangladesh Observer, The New Nation*. Financial dailies: *Financial Express, Bonikbarta, Amader Orthoneeti*	
Electricity	220 volts, 50 Hz	3-pronged plugs
Internet Domain	.bd	
Telephone	Bangladesh's country code is 88.	Large use of cell phones
Time Zone	GMT+5 hours	There is no daylight saving time. Clocks are half an hour ahead of India.

chapter one

LAND &
PEOPLE

Aamar shonar Bangla, Aami tomay bhalobashi.
Chirodin tomar aakash, tomar batash
aamar prane bajay banshi.

My golden Bengal, I love you.
Your sky, your air, always play a sweet
tune in my heart.

[From the national anthem by Rabindranath Tagore]

GEOGRAPHY

Bangladesh is a Southern Asian country, bordering
the Bay of Bengal, between Myanmar (Burma) and
India. It is almost surrounded by India, only a small
part in the southeast having a border with Myanmar.
Bangladesh lies across the Tropic of Cancer, in the
Ganges Delta, where the Ganges (Ganga),
Brahmaputra, and Meghna rivers converge. Most
of the country is situated on the deltas of the large
rivers flowing down from the Himalayas: the Ganges
unites with the Jamuna (the main channel of the
Brahmaputra) and later joins the Meghna to empty
eventually into the Bay of Bengal.

Most parts of Bangladesh are less than 39.4 feet
(12 m) above sea level; the highest point is 4,036 feet

(1,230 m) in the Chittagong Hill Tracts in the southeast. Cox's Bazar, south of the city of Chittagong, has a beach that is unbroken over 77.62 miles (125 km). A large part of the coastline is a marshy jungle, the Sundarbans. This is the largest area of tidal mangrove forest in the world.

Because it is mostly flat and low-lying, the country is prone to annual flooding. However, the numerous rivers and canals, together with the rich alluvial soil deposited by floodwaters, make it very fertile.

LANDSCAPE

Most—more than nine-tenths—of Bangladesh's territory is flat. The areas of hilly terrain are in the Chittagong Hill Tracts and Sylhet, in the southeast and northeast respectively. The mountains and hills running from Chittagong to Sylhet are part of the Arakan Range. There are also some small hills in the district of Mymensingh. The highest peak is officially Keokradong, at 3,235 feet (986 m), in the

remote Bandarban district of Chittagong; however, international bodies have authenticated Saka Haphong in the Mowdok Range on the border with Myanmar as being higher, at approximately 3,488 feet (1,063 m).

There are some man-made lakes, mostly in Chittagong. The biggest is Rangamati/Kaptai Lake, which was created when the Kaptai hydroelectricity plant was built. During the British period, the headquarters of Assam–Bengal Railways were located in Chittagong, and lakes were created to create a water supply for the railway employees and the engines. The largest of these is Foy's Lake, which has been turned into a tourist resort; others are Agrabad Lake and Horse Shoe Lake. There are also some huge natural bodies of water, called *haor*, in the districts of Sylhet and Mymensingh.

The Chittagong Hill Tracts, portions of the north-central Madhupur Tract, and the Sundarbans in the southwestern corner of the country are the principal areas of vegetation. Forested areas, however, amount to less than one-sixth of the total area of the country.

The Sundarbans, lying along the coastline, are part of the world's largest mangrove forests. These beautiful protected forests are home to the Royal Bengal tiger and many other unique flora and fauna. The forest, which has a total area of 3,861 square miles (10,000 sq. km), is shared between the Indian state of West Bengal and Bangladesh, the larger part, of 2,317 square miles (6,000 sq. km), falling within Bangladesh. It earned the distinction of becoming

a UNESCO world heritage site in 1997. The Sundarbans are intersected by a complex network of tidal waterways, mudflats, and small islands of salt-tolerant mangrove forests.

Also in the southern part of the country lies Cox's Bazar, the world's longest sandy sea beach. Gently sloping, it is located 93.2 miles (150 km) south of the industrial port of Chittagong. Cox's Bazar is a seaside resort, a fishing port, and a district headquarters (see page 18).

CLIMATE

Bangladesh has a tropical climate, typical of the Southeast Asian region, with a hot, humid summer, a warm, rainy monsoon season, and a dry, mild winter. January is the coolest month, with temperatures averaging around 78°F (26°C), and April the warmest, with temperatures ranging from 91° to 96°F (33° to 36°C). The climate is one of the wettest in the world. Most places receive more than 60 inches (1,525 mm) of rain a year, and areas near the hills receive 200 inches (5,080 mm). Most rains occur during the monsoon and there is little rain in winter.

Bangladesh has six seasons. It is difficult to match them with the Western calendar, but roughly they are as follows:

- Summer (*Grishmo*): April–June
- Monsoon (*Barsha*): July–August
- Fall (*Sharat*): September–October
- Between Fall and Winter (*Hemanta*): November
- Winter (*Sheet*): December–January
- Spring (*Basanta*): February–March

The winter is mild, although some years in the northern part of the country the winter chill can become quite severe. In the capital city, Dhaka, the average temperature in January is about 66°F (about 19°C), and in May about 84°F (about 29°C). Fall is pleasant and spring is very colorful. Beautiful *Krishnachura* flowers with bright red and yellow petals bloom along with a variety of other flowers.

Bangladesh is subject to devastating cyclones, originating over the Bay of Bengal, in April–May and September–November. Often accompanied by surging waves, these storms can cause great damage and loss of life. The cyclone of November 1970, in which about 500,000 lives were lost in Bangladesh, was one of the worst natural disasters of the twentieth century. This flat, low-lying country is easily flooded. Whenever there are heavy rains and overflowing rivers in the northeastern region of neighboring India, mainly Assam, vast amounts of surplus water run through and inundate extensive areas of Bangladesh.

REGIONS

Bangladesh is divided into seven major administrative areas, called "divisions". Each of these is named after the largest or major city within its jurisdiction, which serves as the administrative center of that division. The seven divisions are: Barisal, Chittagong, Dhaka, Khulna, Rajshahi, Rangpur, and Sylhet.

Each division is further split into districts, or *zilas*, which are then further subdivided into *upazilas*. These are the subdistricts, the lowest tier of district administration under local government. There are sixty-four districts/*zilas* and 500 *upazilas*. The lowest administrative units in rural areas are the union councils, or "unions," with each union consisting of several villages. There are around 64,000 villages in Bangladesh. In the metropolitan areas, police stations cover areas that are divided into wards, which are further informally divided into *mahallas*.

There are no elected officials at the divisional or district levels, and the administration is composed only of government officials. Direct elections are held for each union (or ward), electing a chairperson and a number of members. In 1997, a parliamentary act was passed to reserve three seats (out of twelve) in every union for female candidates.

Dhaka is the capital and largest city of Bangladesh. Those cities with a city corporation are run by an elected mayor. Other major cities, including Mymensingh, Gopalganj, Jessore, Bogra, Dinajpur, Saidpur, Narayanganj, Cox's Bazar, and Rangamati, are run by a municipality headed by a chairman elected by the people. Elections to all local government bodies are held every five years.

THE PEOPLE

Today the people of the region of Bengal, the Bengalis, are politically divided between the nation of Bangladesh and the Indian state of West Bengal. The term Bangladeshi refers to the citizens of Bangladesh, which has been a sovereign state since the 1971 Liberation War.

The Bengali people are not very tall, with black hair and eyes light to dark in color. Skin tones are also light to dark. They are a mix of Indo-Aryan, Austro-Asiatic, and Mongol peoples. Modern Bengalis are a homogeneous but ethnically very

diverse group, with the origins of many people extending as far afield as Tibet and Iran.

Bengalis comprise 98 percent of Bangladesh's total population; the remaining 2 percent include ethnic minorities and non-Bengali Muslims. They possess a rich culture and language—*Bangla*, known to the Western world as Bengali—which is a member of the eastern branch of the Indo-Aryan languages. In their native language, the people are referred to as *Bangali*.

The population is almost evenly distributed throughout its sixty-four districts except for the hilly areas inhabited by ethnic minorities. The population density is 1142.3 per square kilometer (World Bank, 2011 est.). The eastern districts have a slightly higher density than the western ones. The ethnic minority people, who lead a simple life, are generally self-reliant, producing their own food and drink and weaving their own clothes. Almost 80 percent of the country's total population of about 160 million live in the rural areas, where livelihood primarily depends on agriculture.

In Bangladesh, the rate of child mortality per 1,000 has come down to 76.8. The gender ratio is 106 males to every 100 females. About 96.3 percent of families have access to safe drinking water. People are literate, with about 5 million having passed secondary school (high school) level and another 1.27 million being university graduates. The primary school enrollment rate has risen to 86 percent.

The indigenous peoples of Bangladesh are the native ethnic minorities of the southeastern, northwestern, north-central, and northeastern frontier regions of the country. These regions include the Chittagong Hill Tracts, Sylhet Division, Rajshahi Division, and Mymensingh District. The total population of ethnic minorities in Bangladesh was estimated to be over 2 million in 2010. These communities are ethnically diverse.

The census of 2011 shows twenty-seven different ethnic population groups. The largest is the Chakma, consisting of 444,748 people, while the second largest is the Marma, at 202,974. There are other groups or communities, including the Santal, the Garo, the Manipuri, the Tanchangya, the Murong, and the Khasi.

A BRIEF HISTORY

The history of Bangladesh dates back millennia, through the early Stone, Copper, and Bronze Ages, and is inextricably intertwined with that of the rest of the Indian subcontinent. Stone Age tools 20,000 years old have been found in the Bengal region. Remnants of Copper Age settlements date back 4,000 years. The North Indian Iron Age lasted roughly from 1200 to 300 BCE and encompassed much of the Vedic period.

The Vedic Period (c. 1500–272 BCE)

From around 1500 BCE, Bengal was invaded by Aryans, a tribal, semi-nomadic people who had first settled in the northern Indus Valley. The spread of Indo-Aryan civilization threatened to supplant the indigenous language and culture. The original inhabitants of Bengal, the Adivasi, were looked down upon by the Aryans and portrayed as demons and bandits, even though their rich culture and traditions dated back more than a thousand years. Bengal is mentioned in the Vedic epics, the *Ramayana* and the *Mahabharata*.

By the seventh century BCE western Bengal had become assimilated into Indo-Aryan civilization as part of the *Mahajanadapa* (or Great Kingdom) of Magadha, originally based in the area of modern-day Bihar. By 600–500 BCE, the early clan-based societies were evolving into small states. Vedic texts suggest that between the sixth and third centuries

BCE Bengal was divided among various tribes or kingdoms known as the *janapadas*—Vanga (southern Bengal), Pundra (northern Bengal), and Suhma (western Bengal).

Around the fourth century BCE Bengal consisted of small kingdoms. For example, the kingdom of Samatata, ruled by the Chandra and Kharga dynasties, controlled the areas east of the Meghna River, such as Comilla, Tripura, and part of Noakhali. The dates of these early dynasties are only guesswork. Written records started with the arrival of the Greeks.

The Gangaridai Kingdom (c. 300 BCE)
When Alexander the Great invaded the region in 326 BCE, north and west Bengal were part of the Magadhan Empire. To the south, the Gangaridai Empire, situated at the mouth of the Ganges River, was independent and prosperous from overseas trade. Greek and Latin historians suggested that Alexander withdrew from India deterred by the prospect of a counterattack (with war elephants) by the allied forces of the Gangaridai and Nanda Empires. Gangaridai, according to Greek accounts, continued to flourish at least up to the first century CE.

The Vanga Kingdom
(c. 4th century BCE–1st century CE)
The ancient Vanga (Bongo) Kingdom was a powerful seafaring nation. The earliest reference to Vanga as a

territorial unit is found in the fourth-century BCE Sanskrit treatise *Arthaxastra* of Kautilya, in which it is mentioned as an area where the finest-quality white and soft cotton fabrics were produced. References in the *Mahaniddesha* (c. second century CE) and the *Milindapanho* (c. first or second century CE) indicate that there was a coastal area approachable from the sea in the territory of Vanga. From these references, Vanga appears to be an eastern country located in the proximity of the *janapadas* of Pundra, Suhma, Tamralipti, Anga, Mudgaraka, Magadha, and Pragjyotisa. The earliest reference to "Vangala" (*Bongal*) has been traced to the Nesari plates (c. 805 CE) of the Rashtrakuta emperor Govinda III (793–814 CE), which speak of the Pala king Dharmapala as the king of Vangala.

The Maurya Period (321–184 BCE)

In around 321 BCE Chandragupta Maurya conquered the Nanda Empire and founded the Maurya Empire in northern India. This extended from the Bay of Bengal in the east to the Indus River in the west. By the end of his reign in 298 BCE Chandragupta had subjugated almost the entire Indian subcontinent. He was the first emperor to unify India into a single state, and his reign was a time of great social and religious reform. Buddhism and Jainism became increasingly prominent. His grandson, the emperor Ashoka, conquered Bengal in the second century BCE. Under a succession of weaker kings, however, the vast Maurya Empire shrank and finally collapsed when Brihadnatha, the last emperor, was killed by a rival dynasty in 185 BCE.

The Gupta Empire (320–600 CE)
The following period of Bengal's history is obscure.
Bengal consisted of two kingdoms—Pushkarana
and Samatata—until its conquest by Samudragupta
(c. 335–c. 375 CE), the second king of the rising Gupta
dynasty.

Called the "Indian Napoleon"
by historians, Samudragupta
was a military genius who
ushered in the Golden Age of
India. His son Chandragupta
II defeated a confederacy of
Bengali kings, resulting in
Bengal becoming fully integrated
into the great north Indian Gupta
Empire. Chandragupta was a patron of Hindu art,
literature, science, and religion.

During Gupta rule, Bengal became part of a global
trade network. The main groups dominating socioeconomic life were the *Nagarshreshthi* (bankers),
Sarthabaha (merchants), and *Kulik* (artisans).

The Gauda Kingdom (c. 590–637)
Mortally wounded in 450 CE by the Huns from
Central Asia, the Gupta Empire went into decline.
By the sixth century it had largely broken up. Eastern
Bengal splintered into the kingdoms of Vanga,
Samatata, and Harikela. In the west the Gauda
kingdom arose.

Shashanka, a vassal of the last Gupta emperor,
proclaimed independence and unified the smaller
principalities of Bengal (Gaur, Vanga, and Samatata).
During his reign (606–637 CE) he attempted
unsuccessfully to unite all the different kingdoms of
Bengal. He vied for regional power in northern India

with the emperor of Thanesar, Harshavardhana. Shashanka is often credited with the development of the Bengali calendar as the starting date falls squarely within his reign.

Harsha's continuous pressure led to the gradual weakening of the Gauda kingdom, which finally ended with Shashanka's death. After the overthrow of his son Manava, Bengal descended once more into a period of disunity and foreign invasion.

The Pala Empire (750–1174)
The Pala dynasty (c. 750–1174) was the first independent Buddhist dynasty of Bengal. The name *Pala* means "protector" and was used as an ending to the names of all Pala monarchs. Gopala, the first ruler, came to power in 750 in Gaur through democratic election—one of the first democratic elections in South Asia since the time of the Mahajanapadas—and reigned till 770. The dynasty lasted four centuries (750–1120) and ushered in an age of stability, prosperity, culture, and learning. Subsequent rulers expanded the boundaries and made the empire the dominant power in northern and eastern India, much of South Asia, and beyond. The Pala Empire is regarded as Bengal's golden age. The arts flourished, temples were built, and universities were supported.

After peaking under Devapala (810–50), Pala ascendancy ended and several independent dynasties and kingdoms emerged. However,

Mahipala I recovered control of Bengal and expanded the empire further. After him the Pala dynasty again went into decline until Ramapala, the last great Pala ruler, managed to retrieve its fortunes to some extent. In the twelfth century the empire gradually disintegrated, meeting its end in the defeat of the last Pala king, in 1174.

The Sena Empire (1070–1230)

The Palas were ousted by the Sena dynasty in the twelfth century. Vijay Sen (c. 1096–1159), the second ruler of this dynasty, defeated the last Pala king and succeeded in bringing all of Bengal under one unified rule, which continued up to 1204.

The Sena brought about a revival of Hinduism in Bengal. They built temples and monasteries and consolidated the caste system. The fourth king of this dynasty, Lakshman Sen, expanded the empire beyond Bengal to Bihar, Assam, and Odisha. At its peak the Sena Empire covered much of the northeastern region of the Indian subcontinent.

Lakshman was later defeated by the Muslims and fled to eastern Bengal, where he ruled for a few more years.

Islam Comes to Bengal

Bengal was possibly the wealthiest part of the Indian subcontinent until the sixteenth century. Islam made its first appearance there during the ninth century with the arrival of Sufi missionaries and Arab merchants. This was a prelude to the tide of Islam that washed over the country at the end of the twelfth century.

Beginning in 1202, a military commander from the Delhi Sultanate, Mohammed Bakhtiar Khilji, overran Bihar and Bengal as far east as Rangpur, Bogra, and the Brahmaputra River. Although he failed to bring all of Bengal under his control, the expedition managed to defeat Lakshman Sen, who moved with his two sons to a place then called Vikrampur (in present-day Munshiganj District), where their diminished dominion lasted until the late thirteenth century. In 1213 Sultan Giasuddin gained freedom from Delhi and ruled Bengal for twelve years. He was the first independent sultan.

During the fourteenth century, the former Bengali kingdoms became known as the Sultanate of Bengal. It was ruled intermittently by the Sultanate of Delhi, as well as by a loose, independent confederacy of powerful Muslim and Hindu warrior chiefs and landlords known as the *Baro-Bhuiyans*, or the Twelve Feudal Rulers.

Hindu states continued to exist in southern and eastern parts of Bengal till the 1450s. After the collapse of the Sena Empire, the Hindu Deva Kingdom ruled eastern Bengal from its capital at Bikrampur in the present-day Munshiganj District of Bangladesh. Inscriptional evidence shows that this kingdom extended up to the Comilla–Noakhali–Chittagong region.

The Bengal Sultanate
There were five short-lived semi-independent Muslim dynasties in Bengal. The first sultan was Fakhruddin Mubarak Shah, who declared independence from the Delhi Sultanate in 1338 and proclaimed himself Sultan of Bengal in Sonargaon. The sultanate began to disintegrate after the fall of

the Hussain Shahi dynasty in the sixteenth century, and was absorbed into the Mughal Empire in 1576.

Ilyas Shahi Dynasty (1352–1487)
Shamsuddin Ilyas Shah (1342–58) founded a sovereign sultanate in Bengal, free from the hegemony of the Delhi Sultanate. He united the main three states of Bengal—Lakhnauti, Satgaon, and Sonargaon—and took control of east Bengal and Kamrup (part of Assam). He also conquered parts of present-day Uttar Pradesh and Odisha. During this period alien Muslims assimilated totally into Bengali society. Above all, the whole territory, which had never before been known by a single name, came to be designated as *Bangalah*.

His successors successfully repelled Delhi's attempts at recapture and the Sultanate eventually expanded from Khulna in the south to Sylhet in the northeast. The Ilyas Shahi Sultanate lasted for nearly one hundred and fifty years. The Sultans of Bengal developed civic institutions and were receptive to local culture. They were patrons of Bengali literature and created an environment in which Bengali culture and identity could flourish. Though their rule was interrupted by a Hindu uprising under Raja Ganesha the dynasty was later restored by Nasiruddin Mahmud Shah

Hussain Shahi Dynasty (1494–1538)
The Hussain Shahi dynasty was founded by Alauddin Hussain Shah. Considered the greatest of the sultans of Bengal, he presided over a cultural renaissance and was known for religious tolerance toward his Hindu subjects. He extended the sultanate as far as the port of Chittagong, which saw

the arrival of the first Portuguese merchants. His son, Nasiruddin Nasrat Shah, made a treaty with Babur, founder of the Mughal Empire, and so saved Bengal from a Mughal invasion. The last sultan of the dynasty faced rising Afghan activity on the northwestern border. Eventually, in 1538, the capital, Gaur, was sacked by the Afghans, who remained there for several decades until the arrival of the Mughals.

The Mughal Period (1575–1688)

Akbar, the greatest of the Mughal emperors, defeated the Karrani rulers of Bengal in 1576, thus bringing Bengal once more under the control of Delhi. It became a Mughal *subah*, or province, ruled through *Subahdars* (governors). Akbar's progressive rule oversaw a period of prosperity through trade and development in Bengal and northern India.

Dhaka became the capital of the province of Bengal, but due to its geographical remoteness it was difficult to govern, especially the area east of the Brahmaputra River. Bengali ethnic and linguistic identity further crystallized during this period, since the whole of Bengal was united under a stable administration. Furthermore its inhabitants were given sufficient autonomy to cultivate their own customs and literature.

There were also several autonomous Hindu states in Bengal during the Mughal period, such as Jessore and Burdwan. These vassal kingdoms contributed greatly to its economic and cultural landscape. Militarily, they served as the first line of defense against Portuguese and Burmese attacks. Many of them fell during the late 1700s, while Koch Bihar in the north survived until the advent of the British.

The Nawabs of Bengal (1717-1880)

The nawabs of Bengal were the hereditary Subahdars or *nazims* (governors) of Bengal under Mughal rule who later became sovereign rulers of the province. After the death of Emperor Aurangzeb, Murshid Quli Khan (1717–27) became the first independent nawab. Although continuing to recognize Mughal suzerainty and to send annual tribute to Delhi, he laid the foundations of a well-run and economically viable state. His son-in-law, Shuja-ud-Din Muhammad Khan, made the decisive break with Delhi, ushering in a series of independent Bengali nawabs.

From 1717 until 1880, three successive Islamic dynasties—the Nasiri, Afshar, and Najafi—all related by bloodlines, ruled Bengal. Nawab Alivardi Khan routed the forces of the Maratha Confederacy, a rising Hindu imperial power, and crushed an uprising of the Afghans in Bihar. The last independent nawab, Siraj ud-Daula, was killed in the Battle of Plassey against the British East India Company

in 1757, betrayed by his commander Mir Jafar.
The British installed Mir Jafar on the throne and
established themselves as the rulers of Bengal.
The Najafi dynasty continued until 1880.

British Rule (1600–1947)

The first Europeans to reach Bengal were
Portuguese traders and missionaries in the late
fifteenth century. They were soon followed by
Dutch, French, and English trading companies, all
of which set up factory towns. When the Portuguese
began to abuse their position, the Mughal Subahdar
of Bengal crushed them in the Battle of Hoogly
(1632).

During Aurangzeb's reign, the local nawab sold
three villages, including what would become the
port of Kolkata, to the English East India Company.
The Company established a fortified base at Kolkata
(anglicized as "Calcutta") and gradually expanded
its commercial activities and administrative
control. Disputes over trading rights led to the

Anglo–Mughal War (1686–90), in which Shaista Khan, the Nawab of Bengal, defeated the Company army in the battles of Hoogly and Baleshwar and expelled it from Bengal.

In 1757, after the defeat of Siraj ud-Daula and his French allies at Plassey, the East India Company, under the leadership of Robert Clive, returned to Bengal as a political power, effectively governing it on behalf of the British Crown. This decisive victory saw off Britain's European rivals in India and led to the eventual defeat of the Mughals and the consolidation of Company rule over the subcontinent. Calcutta became a major trading port for the bamboo, tea, sugar cane, spices, cotton, muslin, and jute produced in Dhaka, Rajshahi, Khulna, and Kushtia.

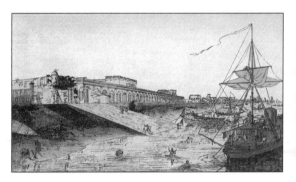

The British rulers introduced a new land tenure system, which had a great impact on the Bengalis. They replaced the old Mughal feudal order with a new social structure and three distinct classes—the *Zamindars* (hereditary landowners), the middle class, and the commoners. They skewed the economy to serve the Company's needs and started transferring the treasure and resources of Bengal to Britain. They raised land taxes, imposed indigo farming on the peasants in place of food crops, and gradually eliminated the production of muslin—a unique hand-woven fabric so fine that you could pass a whole six-yard sari through a finger ring.

Once the Industrial Revolution was under way in England, it became Company policy to halt the production of this fine material and to import English clothing. There are gruesome tales of muslin weavers being tortured and abused by Company officials, businessmen, and the Zamindars' *gomastas* (bailiffs).

In 1773 the East India Company established a capital in Calcutta; appointed its first governor-general, Warren Hastings; raised a native Indian army; and pursued expansionist policies. By 1818 it controlled most of India.

Growing discontent with British rule among the *sepoys*—the Hindu and Muslim soldiers serving in the Company's three armies—culminated in open rebellion in 1857. The scale of the "Indian Mutiny" against the East India Company prompted the British government to intervene. The rebellion was brutally suppressed and in 1858 administrative control of British India was transferred to parliament in Westminster.

The new British "Raj" was organized under a Viceroy

and consisted of provinces directly administered by Britain and semiautonomous princely states under the ultimate authority of the British Crown. The Raj continued the pattern of economic exploitation. Famine, exacerbated by government policy, racked the subcontinent many times, including at least two major famines in Bengal.

The Bengal Renaissance

During the nineteenth and early twentieth centuries a social and cultural reform movement arose in Bengal, the impact of which spread throughout India. There was a flowering of culture: religious and social reformers, scholars, writers of literature, journalists, patriotic orators, and scientists reclaimed Indian culture and teachings and blended them with modern Western thought.

Bengal was one of the most important provinces of the Raj and played a major role in the Indian independence movement, in which clandestine, armed revolutionary groups such as Anushilan Samiti and Jugantar were dominant. Many of the early proponents of the freedom struggle, and subsequent leaders in the movement, were Bengalis. The Bangladeshi people are also very proud of their national poet Kazi Nazrul Islam (1899–1976), greatly remembered for his impassioned activism against the oppression of colonial rule in the twentieth century. He was imprisoned for writing his most famous poem, "*Bidrohee*" ("The Rebel").

The Partitioning of Bengal

Bengal was partitioned twice in the twentieth century, in 1905 and in 1947. These events have marked the psyche of the Bengali people. In 1905 the British divided Bengal for administrative purposes into an overwhelmingly Hindu west, including Bihar and Odisha, and a predominantly Muslim east, including Assam. Dhaka became the capital. Owing to strong agitation, however, the British reunited East and West Bengal in 1912.

In early 1947 Britain announced the decision to end its rule in India. In June the nationalist leaders agreed to the partition of British India into Hindu and Muslim dominions. Bengal was again split into the state of West Bengal, as part of secular India, and the Muslim region of East Bengal under Pakistan, to be renamed East Pakistan. The partition of Bengal entailed the greatest exodus of people in human history. Millions of Hindus migrated from East Pakistan to India, while thousands of Muslims crossed the border into East Pakistan.

East Pakistan (1947–71)

East and West Pakistan were separated by more than 1,000 miles of Indian territory, and almost from the beginning friction began to develop between the two regions. Inequalities between the two soon stirred up Bengali nationalism among the people of East Pakistan, who had little in common with their western counterparts apart from the Islamic faith, and who felt exploited by the West Pakistan-dominated central government. Linguistic, cultural, and ethnic differences also contributed to the estrangement.

In the Pakistan Assembly, members had to speak either in Urdu (the common Indo-Aryan language of northwestern India and Pakistan) or in English. An Assembly member from East Pakistan, Dhirendranath Dutta, brought forward an amendment to include Bengali as a national language, but his proposal was ignored. Then on March 21, 1948, at a meeting in Dhaka, Muhammad Ali Jinnah announced that "Urdu and only Urdu will be the national language of Pakistan." This sparked widespread protests among the Bengali-speaking majority of East Pakistan. Facing rising sectarian tensions and mass discontent with the new law, the government outlawed public meetings and rallies. Immediately the Bengali students protested. They decided it was time to assert their cultural identity. For Bengalis there was no clash between their culture and their religion,

but the Pakistani regime wanted to impose its own identity on them—one based wholly on religion.

The Bangla Language Movement
These events led to the rise of a movement aimed at gaining recognition of Bengali as an official language of Pakistan, which would allow it to be used in government. In 1952, the emerging middle classes of East Bengal (or East Pakistan) organized an uprising known later as the Bangla Language Movement. The East Bengalis were initially agitated by the decision

of the central government of Pakistan to establish Urdu—a minority language spoken only by the supposed elite class of West Pakistan—as the sole national language. Across the country, the police imposed a ruling known as Section 144, which banned any sort of meeting or public gathering.

In defiance of the law, students at the University of Dhaka and other political activists organized a protest on February 21, 1952. Matters reached a climax when the police shot and killed several demonstrators. Bangladeshis still remember the martyrs of the Language Movement—Abul Barkat, Abdus Salam, Rafiq Uddin Ahmed, Abdul Jabbar, Ohiullah (an eight- or nine-

year old boy), and Safiur Rahman—with love and respect. To commemorate the movement, the Shaheed Minar (Martyrs' Monument), a solemn and symbolic sculpture, was erected at the site of the massacre.

This incident was the beginning of a long struggle. The deaths provoked widespread civil unrest. The Language Movement catalyzed the assertion of Bengali national identity in Pakistan and became the forerunner of the Bengali nationalist movement, which was founded mainly by secular students and various political parties. After several years of conflict, the central government relented and granted official status to the Bengali language in 1956.

Pakistan's nascent democratic institutions were subject to military intervention, and the period between 1969 and 1971 was one of martial law. There were protests and a mass uprising against the military regime in late sixties led by the students of East Pakistan, and in 1969 Pakistan's iron man, Ayub Khan, was ousted.

On November 12, 1970, there was a cyclone accompanied by a huge tidal surge along the coastal areas of East Pakistan. One million people died and hundreds of millions of assets were destroyed. But the central government seemed indifferent and showed extreme negligence in rescuing those who were lucky to survive. This behavior greatly increased the grievances of people in East Pakistan. Immediately after the disaster national elections were held all over Pakistan.

Election Victory Denied

In the national elections of December 1970, the Awami League party, headed by the charismatic Sheikh Mujibur Rahman, won a landslide victory, giving it the constitutional right to form the next government. But the political and military establishment of West Pakistan was not ready to hand over power to an East Pakistan-based party, and military president General Yahya Khan postponed the pending session of the National Assembly indefinitely. Violent protests broke out across East Pakistan. The regime started a round-table conference with the Awami League in Dhaka, but behind the scenes they sent troops to quell the rebellion.

The Awami League called a huge public gathering at Dhaka's historic Race Course on March 7, and in an historic speech Sheikh Mujib told Bengalis to prepare for the possibility of a war of independence, and called for a month-long mass civil disobedience campaign throughout the province. Though independence would be officially declared on March 26, 1971, historians agree that his March 7 speech galvanized the nation and gave people the courage to oppose the Pakistan Army.

> "The struggle this time is our struggle for liberation. The struggle this time is our struggle for freedom . . . When we have given blood, we will give more blood. God willing, we will not rest until we have liberated the people of this country."

The War of Independence

War began on the night of March 25, 1971, when the Pakistan Army launched Operation Searchlight against East Bengali civilians, students, intellectuals, members of the political opposition, and dissenting military personnel. Sheikh Mujib was arrested and the political leaders dispersed, mostly fleeing to neighboring India, where they would organize a provisional government. Before his arrest Sheikh Mujib passed on a handwritten note declaring the independence of Bangladesh, which was circulated and broadcast by the captured Kalurghat Radio Station in Chittagong the evening of March 26.

The killing that started in Dhaka at midnight on March 25 spread all over the region. No one was prepared for the scale of the slaughter, which is widely regarded as genocide. The Pakistan Army and its collaborators targeted Hindu communities as well as East Bengali Muslims (who according to them were not true Muslims but "non-believers"). The people of "Bangladesh," as they had started calling the region, took up arms. These untrained, ordinary people—some politicians and student leaders—started a campaign of guerrilla warfare. A government in exile was formed in the village of Baidyanathtola (renamed Mujibnagar) in the district of Meherpur. India helped in this war, arming and training the freedom fighters and sheltering the millions of refugees who fled East Pakistan.

The war was one of the shortest and bloodiest in modern times. The Pakistani army retaliated by using napalm against villages and committing slaughter and mass rape in villages and cities. Thirty million people were displaced. An estimated ten million refugees entered India, whose government had no choice but to intervene militarily When Pakistan launched preemptive airstrikes on key forward airbases and installations in India, India declared war on December 3, and joined forces with the newly formed Bangladesh Army.

During the month of December, Bengali collaborators with the Pakistan army kidnapped scores of prominent teachers, writers, and thinkers, who were taken from their homes and workplaces and killed. Nonetheless, in thirteen days the war was over and the world's 139th country came into existence on December 17, 1972, as the independent Republic of "Bangladesh" (literally, the "Land of Bengal"). Sheikh Mujibur Rahman became the first prime minister in January 1972 after he was released from jail in Pakistan.

GOVERNMENT AND POLITICS

The Constitution of Bangladesh, enacted in 1972, enshrined four fundamental principles— Democracy, Socialism, Nationalism, and Secularism. Unfortunately, economic conditions deteriorated and law and order collapsed. In 1975, after the fourth amendment of the constitution, Sheikh Mujib declared a state of emergency, limiting the powers of the legislature and judiciary, establishing a strong executive presidency, and instituting one-party rule. The new party was called "Bangladesh Krishak Shramik Awami League" (Bangladesh Peasants' Workers' Awami League), or BAKSAL, and all members of parliament and senior civil and military officials were obliged to join it. All newspapers, except for two taken over by the government, were ordered to stop printing.

Some months later Sheikh Mujib was killed with his whole family by army officers. Only his two daughters, Hasina and Rehana, escaped as they were not in the country. The Awami League leader, Khondkar Mushtaq Ahmed, who had conspired against Sheikh Mujibur Rahman and betrayed him, became president, and a few other Awami League leaders also joined the new government. A few days later other leading figures of the Awami League, some of whom had formed the Bangladesh government in exile, were arrested and put in jail. Tajuddin Ahmed, an effective politician who had led the liberation war in the field, was among them. Four of them, including Tajuddin, were killed inside the jail.

Coup and Countercoup

Military coups changed the balance of power in
Bangladesh. Later, in 1977, the military president
Major General Ziaur Rahman, who had also been
a freedom fighter and a sector commander in the
Liberation War, reinstated multiparty politics,
introduced free markets, and founded his own
political party called the Bangladesh Nationalist
Party (BNP). Zia survived as many as twenty-one
coups in his five years in office until he was
assassinated in an attempted coup in 1981.
Vice President Abdus Sattar succeeded him as
acting president. The Chief of Staff, Lieutenant
General Hussein Muhammad Ershad, executed
Zia's assassins and supported the new president,
Abdus Sattar, who led the BNP to victory in
elections in 1982.

The BNP government failed to improve matters,
however, and, taking advantage of its weaknesses,
Ershad seized power in a bloodless coup on March
24, 1982, and proclaimed himself Chief Martial
Law Administrator. He became president on
December 11, 1983.

To improve rural administration, Ershad
introduced the Upazila and Zila Parishad system—a
devolution of power to local authorities—and held
the "first democratic elections for these village
councils" in 1985. He created and became leader of
a new political party, the Jatiya Party, which won the
elections in 1986. In 1987 he launched the Land
Reforms Action Programme, an initiative to
distribute *khas*—unoccupied state-owned land—to
landless families. Ershad was finally forced to resign
in 1990 after a revolt by the major political parties
and the public. However, he still managed to enjoy a

measure of support and was elected as a member of parliament several times.

The Shanti Bahini Insurgency

Against this backdrop, there was continuing instability in the Chittagong Hill Tracts. In 1972 the Parbatya Chattagram Jana Sanghati Samiti (PCJSS), the United People's Party of the Chittagong Hill Tracts, was formed to defend the rights of the indigenous peoples, 100,000 of whom had been displaced without compensation in 1962 by the construction of the Kaptai hydroelectric dam. Bengalis from the plains were encouraged to settle in the tribal areas, which altered the demographic balance. Political differences over rights and autonomy descended into armed conflict in 1977, when the Shanti Bahini, the armed wing of the PCJSS, launched an insurgency against the government of Bangladesh. This continued despite several negotiation attempts until December 1977, when the government and the PCJSS signed the Chittagong Hill Tracts Peace Accord.

The Two Ladies

In 1991 a constitutional referendum restored parliamentary democracy. The BNP leader Khaleda Zia, wife of the assassinated president Ziaur Rahman, became prime minister. But in a few years the electorate grew disenchanted with her government. The opposition called general strikes and some bureaucrats walked out of the administration. Khaleda Zia was obliged to step down and a caretaker government was appointed.

Elections in June 1996 were won by the Awami League led by Sheikh Hasina, daughter of the assassinated Sheikh Mujibur Rahman. Since then Bangladesh has been ruled alternately by coalitions led either by Sheikh Hasina's Awami League or by Khaleda Zia's Bangladesh Nationalist Party (BNP). To improve its prospects the BNP formed a four-part alliance in 1999. This included its former political foe Ershad's Jatiya Party and the Islamic parties of Jamaat e-Islami Bangladesh and the Islami Oikya Jot. In the elections of 2001 the BNP-led coalition won.

After Khaleda had completed her term, there was a political crisis. The Awami League demanded that new voter lists be prepared because the current lists were allegedly flawed, and that the Election Commission, which they considered partisan, be replaced. The president declared a state of emergency and postponed the elections indefinitely. A caretaker government was once more appointed, but was later dismissed by the president at the instigation of the army.

In June 2007, another neutral caretaker government was formed with the backing of the army. Khaleda Zia and Sheikh Hasina were both arrested on corruption charges. The interim administration published a computerized voter list and organized fresh elections for December 2008. The elections, held in the presence of international observers, were regarded as free and fair. A fourteen-party grand coalition led by Sheikh Hasina's Awami League won with an overwhelming majority of more than two-thirds.

The War Crimes Tribunal

One of the reasons for this record win was that the Awami League had promised to bring the war criminals of 1971 to justice. This was long overdue and none of the previous governments had done it, not even the Awami League when they were in power before. The government now set up the Bangladesh International War Crimes Tribunal to investigate and prosecute people suspected of participating in the genocide committed by the Pakistan Army and its local collaborators. Nine leaders of Jamaat-e-Islami, the largest Islamist party, and two of the BNP were indicted for war crimes.

The trials started in 2013. When one of the convicted criminals, Abdul Qader Molla, was given a life sentence and emerged from court giving a two-finger victory sign, the leniency of the ruling outraged many people, especially the younger generation. Protesters gathered in Dhaka's Shahbagh Square and the Shahbagh Movement was born, with the demand that war  criminals who had tortured, killed, and raped innocents be hanged This gathering grew in just a few days to around 30,000 protesters. They demanded the death sentence for Qader Molla and two other political leaders who had been similarly convicted. As the protest movement gathered force, its leaders also called for Jamaat-e-Islami to be banned from politics and for two of its top leaders to be hanged. After initially expressing support for Jamaat-e-Islami, its political ally, the BNP, cautiously welcomed the Shahbagh protest at the beginning.

Counter-protests, demanding the release of those accused and convicted of war crimes, were launched by Jamaat-e-Islami all over the country, leading to riots in which about a hundred people were killed.

The 2013 Shahbagh protests influenced national politics. Later demands included, as well as the banning of Jamaat-e-Islami, a boycott of institutions supporting it or affiliated with it. People also blamed the BNP for supporting Jamaat-e-Islami. Some compared Shahbagh Square with Tahrir Square in Cairo and called the protest the "Bengali Spring." Later a few more war criminals were given death sentences, and Qader Molla's sentence was changed; he was sentenced to death and hanged.

The Awami League government's term finished at the end of 2013 and a general election was held in January 2014, which the BNP chose to boycott. Jamaat-e-Islami had already been banned from taking part. The two leading parties, the Awami League and the BNP, refused to engage in any dialogue, despite many attempts to persuade them.

The elections went ahead with the participation of some smaller parties, and the Awami League again won with an absolute majority. The turnout of voters, at a conservative estimate, was around 20 percent. This was attributed to the tactics of the Jamaat–BNP alliance, established just prior to election day, which included arson and killing. They burned a bus with its passengers in it, and removed fishplates (metal joining bars) from rail tracks, causing some trains to be derailed. On the night before the election five hundred polling centers were torched and some presiding officers were beaten to death. Even so, the Awami League's election victory does not have much credibility.

THE ECONOMY

Bangladesh's economic performance has improved considerably since the introduction of wide-ranging market-oriented economic reforms in the 1990s, with growth in GDP averaging nearly 6 percent in recent years. The economy has remained resilient despite many adverse factors—extreme land scarcity relative to the population, natural disasters, and poor governance. The achievements in certain social development indicators have been even more impressive. Bangladesh has outperformed other low-income countries in South Asia as a whole in female school enrollment, child mortality rates, and other basic health and education outcomes.

Bangladesh still has a largely rural economy; much of its economic growth is generated by agriculture and in the rural non-farm sector—the latter supported by the strong growth of microcredit under the leadership of Nobel laureate Professor Muhammad Yunus of the University of Chittagong and his brainchild, the Grameen Bank. The Bengali word "*grameen*" means rural, and the Bank emerged from a rural development project in 1976 at the village of Jobra in Chittagong district. This was an experimental initiative by Dr. Yunus when he was teaching at Chittagong University, and Jobra village was adjacent to the university campus.

THE GRAMEEN BANK

Muhammad Yunus believes in two basic principles: first, that credit is a human right; second, that the poor know best how to better their own situation. The prize-winning microfinance organization and community development bank that he founded makes small loans, known as microcredit or "grameencredit," to the rural poor without requiring collateral. The system relies on trust and peer pressure within a group to ensure that the borrowers follow through and conduct their financial affairs with discipline, and it encourages borrowers to become savers, so that their local capital can be converted into new loans to others. More than half of the Bank's borrowers in Bangladesh (nearly 50 million) have risen out of acute poverty thanks to their loan. The overwhelming majority of the borrowers are women.

From modest beginnings thirty years ago, the Grameen Bank has developed microcredit into an important instrument in the struggle against poverty. It has diversified into many different fields and become a source of ideas and models for microcredit and microfinance around the world.

Outside agriculture, the main drivers of growth have been small-scale entrepreneurship, garment manufacture, and the export of labor. There is a sizable number of workers employed in small and medium-sized industries and various service sectors. Bangladesh is now second only to China in the global garment export market, albeit with an undiversified industrial and manufacturing base.

RANA PLAZA

In April 2013, a nine-storied building in greater Dhaka, the Rana Plaza, collapsed, killing about 1,129 and injuring 2,515. The search for survivors under the rubble took nineteen days. Most of the victims were garment workers. Visible cracks in the building had been ignored and it collapsed during the morning rush hour.

This was the deadliest accidental structural failure in modern history. After the disaster, the Bangladeshi government, the factory owners, foreign retailers, and international organizations pledged millions of dollars as compensation for the victim's families. More than a year later, owing to disagreement among the parties, the promises remain unfulfilled.

The Rana Plaza disaster sparked an outcry about the dangerous conditions in the garment industry where millions work, most of them women. There was a pledge to improve the state of factories across the country. Safety measures are being improved and stringent standards are being introduced, but a great deal remains to be done.

chapter two

VALUES &
ATTITUDES

Bangladeshis are essentially a traditional and conservative people who follow customs and norms that have been in place for hundreds of years. Honesty and integrity are two of their most appealing traits. They are hardworking and sincere; they are aware of their dignity, but also have a sense of humor. The hierarchical nature of Bangladeshi society can make some people unquestioningly submissive to those in power.

You will generally find the Bangladeshis friendly, cheerful, and hospitable, yet they are a passionate people and can be volatile at times. They are very divided politically, and this volatility can lead to social and political violence. Often their misplaced sense of loyalty can be dogmatic and unreasoning. This political antagonism is so strong that the two leading political parties and their leaders, Prime Minister Sheikh Hasina and leader of the opposition Khaleda Zia, are not ready to talk to each other on matters relating to the greater good of the nation.

NATIONAL PRIDE

As well as being extremely emotional, the Bangladeshis are very patriotic. They have long suffered under foreign rule, and after the partition

of India in 1947 they had to fight for their identity
and independence against the rulers of West
Pakistan. They faced genocide, waged a guerrilla
war, and endured nine months of conflict before
achieving independence as a sovereign country in
1971, so they are justifiably proud and patriotic: they
love their motherland and are very protective of it.
Occasionally they may engage in self-criticism and
joke about themselves, but the moment an outsider
makes an adverse or disparaging comment, they will
protest and defend their country's honor. There are
many differences in ideology and opinion, but when
a crisis arises Bangladeshis set these aside and unite
to face it together.

A significant advantage enjoyed by Bangladesh is
that it is a monolingual country. Apart from some
ethnic minority groups with their own dialects or
languages, everyone speaks and writes in *Bangla*
(Bengali), so there is no communication difficulty.
It is a very homogeneous country in this sense.

IDENTITY, RACE, AND RELIGION
Bangladesh is one of the largest Muslim countries
in the world. About 80 percent of the population are
Muslims. Most are Sunnis, but there is a small Shia
community. Hindus constitute about 12 percent of
the population. Hindus are almost evenly
distributed in all regions of the country, with
concentrations in Khulna, Jessore, Dinajpur,
Faridpur, and Barisal. There are also significant
numbers of Buddhists and Christians. In the
Chittagong Hills, Buddhist tribes form the majority
of the population and their religion is a mixture
of tribal cults and Buddhist doctrines.

Bangladeshis are religious, but not fanatically so. They want to live in harmony with other faiths and have done so for ages. Sadly, some religious groups and politicians are playing games with people's religious and ethnic feelings. In some quarters, those with vested interests try to create divisions based on race, religion, and nationalism among the uneducated. That creates temporary rifts, but people are always aware of their inclusive culture and heritage, and religious or ethnic factionalism cannot seriously poison their hearts.

The rise of religious fundamentalism, encouraged by a few short-sighted and self-seeking politicians, has created some confusion in the minds of many people as to whether their primary identity should be Bengali or Muslim. Because they follow Bengali culture and traditions they are very different from the Muslims of other countries. It should be mentioned that when Islam first came to this region it mingled with the indigenous culture, which was very old, and over the years evolved into a distinctive

local form. The Muslims of this region are mainstream Sunnis who are influenced by Sufism, a liberal, mystical branch of the Islamic faith.

For most Bangladeshis, their religion is Islam and as a nation they are Bengalis. In their minds there is no clash between the two. Any confusion about identity that may occasionally arise is falsely created by groups with vested interests. When someone asks himself or herself, "Who am I?" two questions come up—are they Bengali and Muslim, or are they Bengali and Bangladeshi? This may sound complicated, but the answer is not really that difficult: as a nation, they are Bengali, their religion is Islam, and their nationality or citizenship is "Bangladeshi."

STATUS

Bangladesh is divided into two socictics, rural and urban, and there are clear class divisions between rich and poor in both the urban and the rural populations. Well-off farmers and large landowners enjoy higher status than poor, marginal farmers. In the postwar period, however, the social divide has tended to become blurred. The class system is gradually breaking down because of the increasing mobility of people, as economic conditions persuade large numbers to migrate from villages to nearby towns and cities. Although class distinction still prevails, with good luck many are improving their status. Urbanization is a major cause of this metamorphosis.

Typically, there is a strict hierarchy in the workplace, and there are many people to help officials perform their duties. There are clerical staff who do administrative work, such as drafting letters, and there are orderlies who take files from one official to another, or one department to another, who may also make tea or coffee for the officials and their guests.

In the villages people are close to one another and support each other in difficult times. But in urban areas people tend to be aloof and rather indifferent. Most do not know, or do not want to know, what is happening next door.

WORK ETHIC

Bangladeshis are conscientious and hardworking. Farmers working in their own fields or someone else's start very early in the morning and work until late. Women, too, work in the fields. People know that they have to work hard in order to produce a good crop.

In the cities most people are punctual and perform their duties to the best of their abilities.

They usually report for work on time and put in their assigned working hours. They are dedicated, honest, and committed to their jobs, regardless of whether they are working for themselves or an employer. Inevitably this is not true for everyone and there are exceptions. Sometimes you find an official's chair empty and its occupant missing for a while. Happily this is not the rule: office time is generally maintained and backlogs are rare.

The younger generation of Bangladeshis is very enterprising. Many have started their own businesses and are successful. Previous generations were content to have a safe job, working for others, and very few young people had the courage or initiative to launch a business, however small. Most followed in their fathers' footsteps and joined the same professions. But now, in the post-1971 years, Bangladeshis are thinking differently.

ATTITUDES TOWARD GENDER

Bangladeshi society is basically patriarchal, but women have more rights than in many other Muslim countries. Married women provide especially important links between their husbands' and brothers' families. By Islamic law, a woman inherits a share of her father's property, although not equal to that of the male heirs. A woman begins to gain respect and security in her husband's or father-in-law's household only after giving birth to a son. Mothers therefore cherish and indulge their sons, while daughters are frequently more strictly disciplined and sometimes even neglected. Sons get preference in education and other opportunities.

In the not too distant past, most women's lives remained centered on their traditional roles and they had limited access to markets, education, healthcare, and local government. This lack of opportunity contributed to a pattern of high fertility, which diminished family well-being and contributed to the malnourishment and generally poor health of children,  frustrating educational and other national development goals. In terms of poverty and deprivation, women were always the hardest hit.

But in the post-liberation years the situation has changed. There has been considerable progress in the attitude toward women. The reason is that women have begun to join the workforce in greater numbers, as more and more have access to education. The network of NGOs (non-governmental organizations) has helped to emancipate women in rural areas. The Grameen Bank has also helped in this, as the majority of the recipients of microcredit offered by it are women (see page 48). Women have thus gained some economic freedom, albeit limited, which has improved their status in the family and in society.

ATTITUDES TOWARD OTHER COUNTRIES

Overall, the Bangladeshis are very cordial and friendly toward foreigners. The country shares most of its land border with India—the other next-door neighbor being Myanmar (Burma)—and many Indians live and work there, as do many people from other countries. Most Bangladeshis love India. They go there for vacations and shopping: Indian holiday spots are by and large the first choice of Bangladeshi tourists. Another reason India is so popular with Bangladeshis is medical treatment. All the major hospitals in Kolkata in the Indian state of West Bengal, as well as in cities like New Delhi, Mumbai, Chennai, and Hyderabad, cater to sizable numbers of Bangladeshi patients. Indian goods, music, and films are popular in Bangladesh. But there is resentment, too, in certain quarters. Some of the decisions or actions taken by their big neighbor make some Bangladeshis unhappy, and there are areas of dispute, such as the sharing of river water and the demarcation of the Chitmahal border enclaves. And then there are Islamist and political groups who try to foment anti-Indian feelings among the people.

Similar problems arise with Myanmar, too. The part of Bengal that is now Bangladesh had a long relationship with Myanmar, as Burma was also part of British India. But there is no free flow of tourists between the two countries today and the people do not know much about one another. In recent times, many Rohinga Muslim refugees have entered Bangladesh from Myanmar. Bangladesh has given them shelter, though this continues to give rise to some disputes between these two neighbors.

ATTITUDE TO TIME
There is a saying that Bangladeshis maintain Bangladesh time, meaning that they display a rather

casual attitude toward timekeeping. In many
cases, social gatherings or cultural events don't
start on time. Sometimes, the chief guests do not
arrive on time, or the organizers are not ready.
But this doesn't happen in every walk of life. Many
people try to be punctual at work or for important
business meetings. However, sometimes this is
taken out of their hands. In the capital city, Dhaka,
it is not always possible to arrive on time because
of the atrocious traffic jams during working
hours. This situation is almost becoming
legendary.

If you are visiting someone socially, allow
plenty of time for this relaxed attitude to time.
They will want to chat before serving you tea or
the meal. And after you have eaten, they will want
you to relax and chat some more, and they will
insist on serving you tea or coffee again before
you take your leave. Though the pace of life has
become fast in Bangladesh, people still like to
relax when they are with friends or visitors.

In most cases, workplace attendance is
maintained with strict rules. In the past, you
might have been lucky to find someone at his
desk during normal working hours. But now this
is changing and people are more serious about
timekeeping.

HOSPITALITY

If you meet any foreign tourist who has spent
some time in Bangladesh you are bound to hear
about hospitality. Bangladeshis are among the
most hospitable people in the world.

If you go to someone's house, you will always be offered something to eat or drink. In villages, if you ask for a glass of water it will be accompanied by a piece of *batasa* (a kind of candy made with sugar or traditional date palm jaggery) or something else. Even if the person is poor and their house has been badly damaged in a storm, they will try to be hospitable.

When you meet Bangladeshis and become friendly, they will help you in any way they can, going out of their way to make your stay as comfortable as possible. They will invite you home for a big meal. Unless they do that, they will feel they have not shown you  enough hospitality. You may arrive in Bangladesh as a stranger, but you will always depart as a friend.

chapter three

CUSTOMS & TRADITIONS

THE CALENDARS

In Bangladesh two different calendars are used in everyday life. One is the Western Gregorian calendar, used by government departments and educational institutions. The other is the traditional Bengali calendar, which is followed for almost all other activities, including the sowing and harvesting of crops in rural areas. In cities and towns it is used in some businesses. Shops open their new account books, popularly called *haalkhata*, either on the last day of the year, known as Sankranti, or on the first day of the Bengali New Year—Pohela Boishakh, the first day of the first month, Boishakh, which falls on April 14 or 15 in the Western calendar.

The Bengali calendar is solar, based on the sidereal year as opposed to the tropical year of the Gregorian calendar, and has 365 days. It consists of six seasons of two months each. Because it was officially introduced by the third Mughal emperor, Jalaluddin Muhammad Akbar, to correspond to the Islamic Hijri year 963, or 1556, there is a difference of 593 years between the two systems. Thus, for example, the Bengali year 1421 started in mid-April 2014.

The origin of the *Bongabdo*, or Bangla Year (*Bongo* is Bangla, and *abdo* is year), is still debated. There are two main hypotheses, but neither has been proven to date. Its development is often attributed to Shashanka, King of Gauda, as the starting date falls within his reign (606–637 CE).

The emperor Akbar reintroduced the *Tarikh-e-Elahi*, as the Bengali calendar was initially known, in order to make tax collection in Bengal easier. Until then agricultural taxes had been collected according to the Islamic Hijri calendar, which, being lunar, did not coincide with the harvest seasons and eventually caused farmers severe difficulties by obliging them to pay taxes out of season. In order to reform the system Akbar commissioned the creation of a uniform, scientific, and workable method of calculating days and months. It was the royal astrologer, Aamir Fatehullah Siraji, who developed this improved calendar, which was a major achievement, based on a union of the solar and lunar years. First called *Fasli San* (agricultural calendar) and then the *Bongabdo* (Bangla Year), it was launched on March 10/11, 1584, but it dates from Akbar's ascension to the throne on November 5, 1556.

Akbar ordered all dues to be resolved on the last day of Choitro (or Chaitra), the last month in the calendar. The next day was the first day of the New Year (Bengali New Year), the day for a new opening. On this day shop owners used to distribute sweets to their tenants and customers, and businessmen would commence a *haalkhata* (new financial records book) and lock their old ones. This practice continues to this day. For Bengali traders and shop owners, Pohela Boishakh is *haalkhata* time—an auspicious day to "open" the ledger. They decorate their shops and business centers with flowers and colored paper, and regular customers are invited to attend an evening party. For consumers it may not always be something to look forward to, for *haalkhata* also means the settling of all outstanding debts. Once a purely local festivity, Pohela Boishakh has gradually grown to become a countrywide day of celebration.

IMPORTANT EVENTS, FESTIVALS, AND
NATIONAL HOLIDAYS
The many festivals and celebrations of Bangladesh have given rise to the expression "*baro mashe tero parban*" (thirteen festivals in twelve months). There are also events that are not exactly festivals, but important days that the whole nation observes, such as Shaheed Dibas—Language Martyrs' Day. Not all the festivals are religious. Some are very secular, such as Bengali New Year's Day. Then there are Nabanno Utsab (Harvest Festival) and Basanta Utsab (Spring Festival) on the first day of the month of Falgun (the first month of spring), when young women wear saffron colored saris and decorate their hair with flowers. Nabanno is celebrated with a *mela* (fair) called Nabanna Mela. Villagers and locals from both major religious groups join in the celebrations with equal fervor.

The most prominent and widely celebrated festivals in Bangladesh are Pohela Boishakh (Bengali New Year's Day, also known as Naba Barsho), Independence Day, Victory Day, Eid ul-Fitr, Eid ul-Azha, Moharram, Durga Puja, Buddha Poornima, and Christmas.

THE BENGALI YEAR

Months

The names of the Bengali months are derived
from the names of stars or constellations:

Boishakh from *Vishakha* (Libra) – 31 days
Jyaistha from *Jaistha* (Scorpio) – 31 days
Asadh from *Asadha* (Sagittarius) – 32 days
Shravan from *Shravana* (Aquila) – 31 days
Bhadra from *Bhadrapada* (Pegasus) – 31 days
Ashvin from *Ashvini* (Aries) – 31 days
Kartik from *Krttika* (Taurus) – 30 days
Agrahayan from *Agraihani* (Aldebaran, or
Alpha Tauri) – 29 days
Paus from *Pusya* (Cancer) – 29 days
Magh from *Magha* (Regulus, or
Alpha Leonis) – 30 days
Falgun from *Falguni* (Leo) – 30 days
Choitro from *Chitra* (Virgo) – 30 days

Days of the Week

These are similar to those in the Western
calendar with Bengali names:

Rabi (Sun) Sunday
Som (Moon) Monday
Mangal (Mars) Tuesday
Budh (Mercury) Wednesday
Brihaspati (Jupiter) Thursday
Shukra (Venus) Friday
Shani (Saturn) Saturday

Shaheed Dibas

Martyrs' Day, on February 21, is an official holiday
observed throughout the country to honor those who
laid down their lives during the Language Movement
protests in 1952. All the subsequent movements in
Bangladesh, including the struggle for independence,
owe their origins to this historic event. The
commemorations center on the Shaheed Minar
(Martyrs' Monument) in Dhaka, symbol of the
people's sacrifice for Bangla, their mother tongue.
Mourning ceremonies begin with a procession called
Probhat Feri at midnight with the song *Amar bhaiyer
raktay rangano ekushay February* ("21 February: The
Day Stained with My Brothers' Blood"). The entire
nation pays homage to the martyrs by placing floral
wreaths at the Shaheed Minar.

This day was declared International Mother
Language Day by UNESCO in 1999. It began being
observed in 2000, and in a resolution in 2008 the UN
General Assembly called upon member states "to
promote the preservation and protection of all
languages used by peoples of the world." By the same
resolution it proclaimed 2008 as the International

Year of Languages, to promote unity in diversity and international understanding through multilingualism and multiculturalism.

Pohela Boishakh (First Day of Boishakh), or Naba Barsho (Bengali New Year)

Pohela Boishakh, usually held on April 14, is the first day of the Bengali calendar and is a public holiday. Because the month of Boishakh ushers in the beginning of the new agricultural season in Bengal the festivities connected with it originally had a rural flavor. These have now evolved to become vast events in the towns and cities, especially in Dhaka, and are among the most spectacular and appealing celebrations in the world.

The Bengali New Year is celebrated throughout the country with colorful day-long gatherings, cultural programs, and the consumption of traditional *panta bhat* (a watery cold rice dish). There are tournaments and boat races in towns and villages. Fairs are held in Dhaka and other towns and in villages. The day had always been celebrated in a smaller way, but after 1962 it started gaining in importance. By 1964 it had become a truly national event and Naba Barsho (*naba* new, *barsho* year) was declared a national holiday.

In Dhaka, even newspaper offices remain closed for the occasion. The festivities begin at daybreak with crowds gathering under a big tree in Ramna Green Park. Elsewhere people find any bank of a lake or river to witness the sunrise. Artists perform songs to usher in the year, particularly Rabindranath Tagore's well-known *Esho, hey Boishakh* ("Welcome, O Boishakh"). A huge part of the festivities in the capital is the procession organized by the students

and teachers of Dhaka University's Institute of Fine Arts. People dress in traditional Bengali costume. Women wear woven cotton saris with their hair bedecked with flowers. The saris and dresses have a theme—red and white in color. Similarly, men wear traditional *panjabis* or *kurtas* (loose, full-sleeved collarless shirts or tunics).

Pohela Boishakh celebrates the simpler, rural roots of Bengal and is a totally inclusive holiday, enjoyed by everyone regardless of class, race, or religion. Homes are thoroughly scrubbed and cleaned; people bathe early in the morning and dress in new clothes. They spend much of the day visiting relatives, friends, and neighbors and go to fairs where agricultural produce, traditional handicrafts, toys, cosmetics, and sweets are sold. The fairs also offer popular entertainment, with singers, dancers, and traditional plays and songs. There used to be horse racing, ox races, bullfights, cockfights, and pigeon racing as well as boat races.

All the gatherings and fairs feature a wide spread of Bengali delicacies. Social and cultural organizations celebrate the day with cultural programs. Newspapers bring out special Naba Barsho supplements, and there are special programs on radio and television channels. In the days leading up to the holiday, there are seasonal discounts on clothes, furniture, and electronics, and various deals and shopping discounts, and the line of festive cotton saris, white with red print, border and embroidery, goes on sale.

There are, of course, special dishes for Pohela Boishakh. Household kitchens exude the aroma of freshly prepared delicacies, especially sweet dishes, because it's thought to be a good omen to start the year (or anything) with *mishtanna* or traditional sweets. The New Year lunch contains various preparations of fish and rice. At open-air celebrations, *panta bhat* (cold rice soaked in water and mixed with chopped onions and chilies and eaten with vegetables and fried fish) is sold.

Don't forget to wish your Bengali friends "*Shubho Naba Barsho!*" ("Happy New Year!") on Pohela Boishakh.

A small number of people sometimes complain that the Bengalis, especially the younger generation, are fast forgetting the traditional ways of celebrating Naba Barsho. But these fears are belied by the enthusiasm that all people, both young and old, display. Everyone loves to wear new clothes on this day, and to exchange sweets and pleasantries with friends and acquaintances. Younger people still touch the feet of their elders and seek their blessing for the coming year. Near-and-dear ones send gifts and greeting cards to each other—these are often handmade and based on local themes, or they may be expensive brands.

Hindus in Bangladesh also celebrate the year's end, or Choitro Sankranti (Choitro/Chaitra, as we have seen, is the last month in the Bengali calendar), with some exciting fairs and festivals such as Gajan and Charak Puja.

Panjika, the Bengali Almanac

As the old year draws to a close, Hindu, and some Muslim, Bengalis throng the bookstalls to buy copies of *Panjika*, the Bengali almanac. This is a rather fat year-long handbook to help you find festival timings, favorable days, and auspicious dates for anything from a wedding to a housewarming, from starting a journey to launching a business, and more. The *Panjika* comes in several sizes: directory, full, half, and pocket. *Panjikas* have come of age with innovative content like the phone numbers of hospitals, doctors, and police stations, religious festival timings for people living abroad—in the United States, Britain, or anywhere else—all in local time, and they sell like the proverbial hot cakes in the Bengali diaspora. Although the Western calendar has gained precedence over the Bengali calendar for conducting day-to-day business, almost all events in rural Bangladesh take place according to the Bengali calendar.

Eid ul-Fitr
The dates of Muslim festivals are calculated according to the lunar Islamic calendar. Eid ul-Fitr, the most important religious festival for Muslims

everywhere, is held on 1 Shawwal, the day after Ramadan, the month of fasting. In Dhaka big congregations worship at the National Eidgah, a huge open field, and at many other mosques and fields.

The joyful celebrations of Eid have become part of the culture of Bangladesh and today it is more of a social than a religious festival. The government declares a three-day holiday, and public transport leaving from the major cities becomes very crowded as people return to their villages or hometowns to be with their relatives.

On the morning of Eid day, prayers of thanksgiving are held all over the country in designated open areas like fields or inside mosques. After the prayers, people greet each other warmly by embracing (*kolakuli)* and saying "*Eid mubarak*" (the equivalent of "Happy Eid"), then return home or visit each other's homes for a celebratory daytime meal, the first in a month. Men embrace each other in this way throughout the day. It is also customary for junior members of the family to touch the feet of the seniors, who return the gesture with blessings (sometimes accompanied by a small sum of money

as a gift). In rural areas, Eid is observed with great fanfare. In some places there are Eid fairs. Sporting events are held, including boat races, *kabaddi*, and other traditional Bangladeshi games, and modern games like cricket and football (soccer). In urban areas, people play music, visit each other's houses, and eat special foods such as *pulao*, *korma*, *biryani*, and sweets made with vermicelli or semolina. Radio and television channels air popular family programs for three or four days for this occasion. Newspapers bring out special supplements.

Eid ul-Adha

The second most important religious festival is Eid-ul-Adha, held on Dhul-Hijjah 10–12. This celebration is similar to Eid ul-Fitr in many ways. The big difference is the *Qurbani*, or sacrifice of domestic animals, in commemoration of the testing of the Prophet Abraham/Ibrahim even to the point of sacrificing his son. At God's command his son was spared and a lamb was provided for sacrifice instead. Numerous temporary marketplaces of different sizes called *haat* operate in different areas for the sale of *Qurbani* animals (usually cows and goats). On the morning of Eid day, immediately after prayers, those who can afford it slaughter the chosen animals. After the ritual a large portion of the meat is given to the poor, and the rest to neighbors and relatives.

Although religious doctrine allows the sacrifice at any time over a period of three days starting from Eid day, most people prefer to perform it on the first day. The public holiday spans three days and many people from the big cities take the opportunity to visit their ancestral villages to share the festival with friends and relations.

Muharram

On the tenth day of Muharram, the first month of the Islamic calendar, very devout Shia Muslims commemorate the martyrdom of the Prophet Muhammad's grandson, Imam Hussain, on this day at the battle of Karbala in Iraq in 680. A large, mournful ceremonial procession sets forth from the Hussaini Dalan Imambara (*imambara* being the house of the Imam) in the old part of Dhaka, winds its way through the streets, and terminates at a place designated as Karbala on the banks of the Dhanmandi Lake. Also *latikhela* (stick fights) are held as reminders of the battle between the troops of Imam Husain and the Umayyad Caliph Yazid.

The tenth day of the month of Muharram (Ashura) is a national holiday in Bangladesh.

Durga Puja

Durga Puja, the biggest festival of the Hindu community, celebrates the victory of the Hindu goddess Durga over the demon Mahishasura, epitomizing the victory of good over evil. Held in autumn, the festival lasts for five days, and culminates on the last day with statues of the goddess Durga being immersed in rivers. In Dhaka big celebrations are held at the Dhakeswari Temple, where a fair is also held, and at the Ramakrishna Mission. Throughout the country *puja mandaps* (pavilions of  different designs) are set up in villages, towns, and cities. Durga Puja is a national holiday.

Christmas

Christmas, popularly called *Boro Din* ("Big Day")
in Bengali, is celebrated by Bengali Christians with
pomp in Dhaka and elsewhere in the country.
Several day-long large gatherings are held at St.
Mary's Cathedral at Ramna, the Portuguese Church
at Tejgaon, the (Protestant) Church of Bangladesh
on Johnson Road, Dhaka, and the Bangladesh
Baptist Sangha at Sadarghat, Dhaka. Events include
the illumination of the churches, decorating
Christmas trees, and the preparation of seasonal
Christmas foods. It is a national holiday.

Buddha Purnima

Buddha Purnima, the most important religious
festival of the Buddhist community, is observed
on Boishakhi Purnima, the day of the full moon
in Boishakh (mid-April to mid-May). It
commemorates Gautama Buddha's birth, attainment
of enlightenment (*nirvana*), and death (his
attainment of *parinirvana*, beyond the cycle of
existence). It is celebrated across Bangladesh with
traditional enthusiasm and solemn devotion.

The day's events start with the hoisting of the
national and religious flags above all monasteries at
dawn, and the chanting of verses from the *Tripitaka*,
Buddhist sacred texts written in Pali. To mark the
day, homes are decorated with flowers and incense is
burned. The Buddhist community organizes various
programs, including colorful processions and
discussions.

Buddha Purnima is a public holiday. Newspapers
devote special features to it while Radio Bangladesh,
Bangladesh Television, and private TV channels air
programs highlighting its significance.

Independence Day and Victory Day
March 26 marks the declaration of the Independence of Bangladesh, and December 16 celebrates the surrender of the Pakistani army and signing of the treaty between India, Pakistan, and the newly formed country of Bangladesh. These are the biggest State festivals, and Dhaka and all other cities and towns put on a grand festive dislay. Both days are public holidays.

On Independence Day, the citizens of Dhaka wake up early in the morning to the booming of guns heralding the occasion. Citizens, political leaders, government officials, socio-political organizations, and freedom fighters place floral wreaths at the Shaheed Minar or the National Martyrs Monument at Savar on both days. There are military parades and speeches, people have picnics, and in the villages there are boat races and wrestling. The Bangla Academy, the Bangladesh Shilpakala Academy (National Academy of Fine and Performing Arts), and other cultural bodies stage concerts, exhibitions, and performances of song, dance, and poetry. At night the main public buildings are illuminated, giving the capital city a

dazzling look. Similar events are arranged in other parts of the country.

Rabindra and Nazrul Jayanti

The birthdays of the Nobel laureate Rabindranath Tagore on Boishakh 25 (the second week of May) and that of the National Poet Kazi Nazrul Islam on Jyaistha 11 (the last week of May) are observed throughout the country. The anniversaries of their deaths are also marked in the same way, with big gatherings, and song and poetry recitals organized by leading cultural organizations.

Rabindranath Tagore is the composer of the national anthem of Bangladesh and he is the only poet in the world who has written the national anthems of two sovereign countries, the other country being India.

There are other, smaller, religious festivals that are observed by Bengalis

throughout the year, such as Shab-e-Barat and Kali Puja (see page 81).

FAMILY CEREMONIES AND TRADITIONS

Social customs surrounding important occasions like birth, marriage, the naming ceremony, and death have a distinct Bangladeshi flavor, with each ethnic and religious group having its own unique way to mark these life events. Bangladeshis are very bound up with folk traditions that have been in existence since pre-Islamic times, which are shared by people of all faiths.

A wedding, of course, is a big social event; other family occasions are a child's first meal of solid food, birthdays, the bride or groom's favorite meal at their parents' or another relative's house before the wedding, or a woman's favorite meal when she is seven months pregnant. And there are the rituals that are performed following a death in the family.

Weddings

Bangladeshi wedding traditions have evolved comprehensively in the past few decades in line with contemporary trends. Online matchmaking has replaced the role of *ghotoks*, the traditional matchmakers. Wedding fashions, cards, decoration, and food have become more cosmopolitan, reflecting modern-day culture. However, the wedding ceremony itself, the centuries-old prenuptial ceremonies, the role of elders, and the post-wedding rituals continue as before. True to the traditional Bangladeshi wedding extravaganza, today's weddings are spread over several days and include many rituals. These begin with engagement ceremonies called *Paan-Chini* (literally, betel leaf and sugar, or sweets).

The *Gaye Holud* ceremony is held at both the bride's and the groom's houses. The groom's family visit the bride and bring her gifts, including jewelry, saris, and traditional presents. The bride touches the feet of the elders and sits on the ground on an elevated platform. First the senior members of the family (sometimes the mother) and then others anoint her face and body with turmeric paste brought by the in-laws. The same happens to the groom in his house. On these occasions the women wear saffron, yellow, or green colors. Both ceremonies are followed by a sumptuous feast. Then the bride's hands are decorated with *mehendi* (henna). Nowadays the henna ceremony is frequently held separately—influenced by Indian (Bollywood) movies.

On the day of the wedding, the groom comes to the bride's house. At first the bride and groom sit in separate rooms, surrounded by their relatives. A *kazi*, a Muslim registrar, goes to each one separately and asks for their consent and declares the marriage solemnized. The marriage is registered with the signing of the marriage contract. The contract states the *mehr*, monetary compensation or a bride price, to be paid by the groom. The formal documents (*kabinama*, or *nikanama*) are also signed in the presence of witnesses. Then the bride and groom sit together and a mirror is placed in front of them. The groom has to look at the bride's image in the mirror and praise her beauty in romantic words. They feed sweets to each other, and exchange rings and fresh flower garlands. Music, dance, and feasts follow the wedding ceremony.

The reception (*bou bhat* or *walima*) is held at the groom's house on the next day or one or two days later. It is again a lavish display of fashionable attire, decoration, entertainment, and food. These are

Muslim wedding customs; Hindu weddings have many more complicated rituals that are followed.

There is a distinctive contemporary flavor to traditional Bangladeshi weddings today. While the women continue to dress traditionally, the men and children prefer Western outfits and fashionable clothes. At wedding feasts *biryani* is still the most popular choice, but for some the menu goes well beyond the traditional rice and fish and includes Indian, Chinese, and European dishes. The entertainment now includes Western dances and film songs as well as traditional music. Gone are the days when the bride and groom were not allowed to meet before their wedding. Now they talk on their cell phones and even go shopping together. Though the wedding ceremony still remains unchanged, the surrounding celebrations bear little relation to the customs of the past and have changed to reflect changing times.

Marriage is a civil contract rather than a religious sacrament in Islam, and the parties to the contract represent the interests of their families rather than their own personal interests or desires. In Bangladesh, parents ordinarily select spouses for their children, although these days there are lots of love marriages. Marriage is generally made between families of similar social standing, although financial standing has come to outweigh family background in the twenty-first century.

Aaiburo Bhat

Before the wedding, the bride- and groom-to-be each have a meal consisting of their favorite foods at their respective homes or at a relative's house. Sometimes this is the last meal they will have at home, or at a close relative's or friend's home, before they are married. It is called the *Aaiburo Bhat* ("virgin meal"). Their favorite dishes are cooked, and family, relations and friends gather for the occasion. The bride or groom eats first, and then everyone joins the feast.

Shadh

When a woman is in her seventh month of pregnancy it is the custom to feed her whatever she craves. This is called *Shadh*, or desire. Again her family, relatives, and friends gather for the occasion. She eats first and then everyone joins in. They also bring her gifts such as saris, jewelry, or cosmetics.

Ceremonies for Children

When a child is born, there will be two ceremonies within the first year of his or her life. First is the naming ritual, a traditional religious ceremony called *Aqiqah*. This used to entail shaving the child's hair off, but this is no longer done by everyone. There is a sacrifice of a goat—two for a boy, one for a girl—and there is a feast on the same day for family and friends.

Then, at about seven months, when the child is old enough to take solid food, there is a ceremony called *Mukhe Bhat* (first rice in her/his mouth). For Hindu families the name of this ceremony is *Annaprashon*. As usual friends and families gather with gifts for the child, who is ceremoniously fed some rice, a piece of meat, or some other suitable food. Then everyone else enjoys a feast. In urban areas, children's birthdays are also celebrated.

Funerals

When someone dies, relatives, friends, and neighbors visit the bereaved family to give their condolences. Some people provide food for three days as the family is not supposed to use fire or cook. If you know the person or a member of his or her immediate family, you can visit them and pay your condolences. You don't need to bring anything; just remember not to wear any bright clothing.

These are the rituals that are observed following a Muslim's death. The body is laid on a bier, with the head facing the *qiblah* (the direction of the *Ka'aba* in Mecca), and washed. It is then wrapped in a *kafan* (an unstitched white cotton shroud) and taken to a mosque or an open field for a special prayer called *janaza.* At the burial the mourners throw a handful of earth into the grave while reciting verses from the Koran. Only men are allowed to attend this ceremony—women are not allowed to go to the graveyard. They can visit afterward, on occasions such as the anniversary of the death or on Eid day.

Muslims bury the body promptly as they believe the soul of the person will suffer if there is a delay. But these days, the body is sometimes kept in a morgue until children, brothers, or sisters can arrive from abroad. After the funeral, no food is offered.

On the third day, relatives, friends, and neighbors gather for funeral prayers and a meal, followed by the distribution of food to the poor. On the fortieth day (*Challisha*) after the death, family members hold a feast followed by special prayers of remembrance.

Hindus cremate the body and also have set rituals on certain days after a person dies; these vary according to caste.

RELIGION

Although the majority of Bangladeshis are Muslims, you cannot draw an exact parallel with other Islamic countries. The beauty of Islam is that in different countries it has evolved and mixed with the local cultures and traditions and assumed different forms. In Bangladesh it has absorbed local customs that do not exist in other Islamic countries. Religion has undoubtedly played an important role in shaping the norms and traditions of Bangladesh and there are clear Islamic influences in everyday life. This can be seen in the greeting "*Assalamo alaikum*" ("Peace be unto you") when Bangladeshis meet each other and the valediction "*Khoda hafiz*" ("God protect you") when they depart.

Muslims in Bangladesh celebrate the joyous festivals of the two Eids, Eid ul-Fitr and Eid ul-Adha (called Eid ul-Azha locally); the fast of Ramadan (or Ramzan); and the two special nights of Shab-e-Qadr ("The Night of Power," the holiest night of the year, during the month of Ramadan, when the first verses of the Koran were revealed to the Prophet) and Shab-e-Barat ("The Night of Salvation," or "The Night of Good Fortune"), during which one's fate is determined, when devout believers spend the night in prayer asking for forgiveness).

Hindus in Bangladesh celebrate Durga Puja, Kali Puja (worship of Kali, goddess of death, time, and change), and Janmastami (the birthday of Lord Krishna). The Buddhists celebrate Buddha Purnima, and the Christians Christmas and Easter.

These are just a few of the religious festivals and feasts that Bangladeshis celebrate. During Ramadan there is a different atmosphere—it is at the same time solemn and joyous. The fast is broken at dusk with a meal called *iftar*. You can see many *iftari* vendors on almost

every street. Every household also prepares the main meal.

The Eids, Pujas, and other religious celebrations are special for everyone. All the religious communities join in one another's festivals, which have become social occasions too, and enjoy the harmony that traditionally exists among the people of Bangladesh.

FOLKLORE
Bangladeshis identify with the ancient folk tradition of Bengali culture. This includes belief in shamanism and the powers of *fakirs* (holy men who are exorcists and faith healers), *ojhaa* (shamans with magical healing powers), and Bauls (wandering minstrels who are followers of the Sufi tradition). There is a strong tradition of music, dance, and literature that embraces both classical Hindu and Muslim cultures. This music involves mostly song and a few instruments that differ from the sophisticated musical instruments of the city. Folk musicians use the one-stringed *ektara*, the mandolin-like *dotara*, the *dhol* (a double-headed drum), the *madol* drum, and the *banshi* (bamboo flute).

The Singer and the Song
The stories told in this music have no specific religious theme. They reflect Sufism and the concerns of everyday life, nature, and human emotions. Some speak about the village maiden beseeching the *majhi* (boatman) to go to the village of her parents and tell them to bring her home for a visit because she is missing them, or asking a bird to take a message to her lover. They have sad tunes, and

paint a social picture for the listeners. Mostly they talk of separation. Sometimes the songs are about going to the holy city of Madina (Medina), or they praise the Prophet Muhammad. They may also describe the love of Radha and Krishna, characters from Hindu mythology whose love for each other also expresses spiritual truths and feelings.

Baul songs are both mystical and at the same time very human. Their simple lyrics promote universal human values. Sometimes the love story in the song has a spiritual undertone.

The most famous Baul folk singer and composer was Lalon Shah (reputedly 1774–1890), whose songs

are popular among Bengalis wherever they live—in Bangladesh, Indian Bengal, Europe, the Americas, the Middle East, or Africa. No one knows whether he was a Hindu or a Muslim. His songs are very spiritual, and many mock divisive identity politics. In simple yet moving language he spoke about the equality and common humanity of all people.

Jatra

A traditional Bengali form of entertainment is *jatra*, a kind of folk theater or open-air opera performed in towns and villages at *melas* (fairs) or at a particular celebration. The *jatra* is held in an open space, on a platform with no curtain, and the audience sits around the stage. The actors use exaggerated gestures and declamation. Until the 1970s there were no female actors; men used to play the female parts. Most performances are of historical plays, with a vague sense of nationalism and patriotism, but there are melodramatic social plays too.

A *jatra* performance begins late in the evening and often continues until just before daybreak. Music and songs dominate the show. Musical instruments include the *dhol* or *dholak* (drums), *mandira* (a pair of metal bars used for rhythmic effect like bells) and *karatal* (cymbal), *banshi* (bamboo flute), and *khol* (also a kind of drum). The *adhikari*, who is actually the manager-conductor, plays the role of the narrator, explaining and commenting on the songs and linking the scenes, often extemporizing.

There are more than two hundred registered *jatra* groups in Bangladesh but only a few are active today. Demand has diminished in the present cultural climate. Protests by radical religious groups have led the authorities to refuse permission to stage shows, and many skilled and talented people involved with *jatra* have become jobless or changed their profession. A change in audience taste is another reason for its decline in popularity.

SUPERSTITIONS

Superstitions are widespread and may differ between north and south Bangladesh or in different districts. Many old customs and beliefs have been passed down through the generations, not so much by teaching as through their widespread practice in everyday life. Some are expressions of a mother's love for her children, or for the well-being of her husband

Thus, when a baby is born, a black kohl spot is put on its forehead to ward off any evil eye. Many people wear a *tabiz* (amulet), or hang it around the neck or arm of their child, as a protective charm. Or they may hang it in their car or in the house to keep away the evil eye.

SOME COMMON SUPERSTITIONS

- You should not cut your nails after dark; it may bring you bad luck.
- If a growing child is lying on the ground, you should not step over them as they will not grow any more.
- If your right palm is itching, you will receive some money; in the case of the left hand money will go out.
- If a comb falls from your hand on to the floor, you can expect some guests.
- Right eye twitching means good luck, left eye means bad luck.
- Do not sit with your head supported on the palm of your hand while resting your elbow on the table; it means you will have a bad life in the future.
- If a shoe or sandal is upside down, turn it over immediately, otherwise it will bring bad luck to the household.
- If a dog is whining in the middle of the night, it means something terrible is coming.
- Muslims have a superstition that you should not stand under a tree in the evening because then the *jinns* (spirits) will get you.

chapter four

MAKING FRIENDS

In Bangladesh good friends are closer and more present in each other's lives than in the West. They tend to call without notice and are more like family, even having a say in important life decisions. In modern Bangladesh, especially in urban areas, friendship between men and women is also quite common—unusual in a Muslim culture. Normally this bond is strongest between people of the same age group. As anywhere, it may be forged in childhood with neighbors or classmates, or later in one's professional life.

Bangladeshi friends love spending time together—to have *adda* (chatting together) whenever possible, to go shopping together, or just to go to each other's houses and share meals. The relationship is lifelong, and even if they live

far apart and do not see each other for ages it remains intact. When they meet again, they simply pick up from where they left off. If there is a wedding or a bereavement, their friends will fly thousands of miles to be with them. They feel responsible for each other's well-being. This deep relationship might sound excluding, but Bangladeshi friendship circles are not closed and foreigners can earn acceptance after a short while.

ATTITUDE TOWARD FOREIGNERS

Many foreigners visit and live in Bangladesh, some of them for years. Apart from tourists, people from many countries are there on business, in diplomatic circles, or with NGOs. Some are simply there with their spouses.

Bangladeshis are quite friendly toward foreigners and at the same time curious. Sometimes you may find young people following you on the streets. Don't be alarmed—they only want to know about you. Generally people treat foreigners as very special guests or friends, and are quite generous toward them. They will look after you, and try to make you comfortable. They

may invite you for a meal, show you around, entertain you, even try to pay at restaurants and similar places. Shopkeepers will offer you tea or cold drinks. Language can be a barrier as Bangladesh is a monolingual country and not everyone can speak English or another foreign language. But they won't allow that to deter them. They will attempt to communicate with their limited linguistic skills and with gestures. If you reciprocate by trying to understand them, you can find good companions, maybe even a friend.

MAKING CONVERSATION

Bengalis do not start a conversation with remarks about the weather as some other cultures do. They will ask about your welfare and whereabouts. They will want to know about you, your country, your people, what you are doing in Bangladesh. They may ask personal questions that by Western standards seem intrusive or indiscreet, unaware that this may seem rude or an encroachment on your privacy. They will ask your name, which country you are from, how old you are, whether you are married and have children, and if not, why not. They don't think it is rude to ask about your salary. Do not be put off by this. Just take people at face value. When their curiosity is satisfied, they will be happy and may become good friends.

Bangladeshis love discussing politics, whether local or international. But you may find them careful or reticent about this subject, both with you and among themselves, as Bangladeshi society is quite divided politically. Apart from this there are no particular areas that are taboo.

Getting Started

You can start with a smile, which will take you a long way. Mastering one or two Bengali phrases, such as how to greet a person or how to ask about his or her welfare, can also help a lot. Remember to show respect when starting a conversation, particularly toward elders and women. Though most people in urban areas can speak some English, that is not the case in villages. When meeting a Bangladeshi for the first time, you can extend your hand to shake a man's. With women you should wait to see what they do. If they extend a hand, you can shake hands, otherwise you can nod, smile, or just say "Hello" or "*Assalamo alaikum*" ("Peace be unto you"), the traditional greeting for Muslims. The response to this is "*Wa alaikum salam*" ("And unto you, peace"). When parting company, you can simply say "Goodbye," or, even better, "*Khoda hafiz*," which means "May God protect you."

MEETING BANGLADESHIS

One can get to meet Bangladeshis in various ways. Through your work is one of them. There are also many clubs in the capital. Apart from purely local clubs, such as the Dhaka Club, the Gulshan Club, or the Uttara Club, where you can only go with a member, there are others that you can join easily. These are mostly expat clubs, such as the British Club, the German Club, the Dutch Club, the Nordic Club, the International Club, and so on, where the food and drink is also less expensive than in the big hotels. The most popular place to meet people is the golf clubs. You can meet Bangladeshis through friends at these clubs and also at social events such as parties or cultural functions.

Forms of Address

Forms of address reflect the hierarchical nature of Bangladeshi society. Bangladeshis append a suffix (or occasionally a prefix) to a person's name to denote respect and the level of closeness between two people. In general, age dictates the form used. If people are of the same age, they use first names. If the person being addressed is older than the speaker, that person is called by their first name and a suffix denoting a particular family relationship, even if they are not actually related. For example, if Junaid is a few years older than the person addressing him, he will be called Junaid *Bhai* (Brother Junaid), or if Hasina is much older than the person addressing her, she will be called Hasina *Khala* (Aunt Hasina).

As a foreigner you can safely address people using Mr./Mrs./Miss/Ms. before their surnames. When you become closer, you can call them by their first names.

DRESS

Bangladeshi women widely wear elegant and colorful saris, pronounced and spelled *sharees*. In urban areas some wear Western clothes. These days the *salwar kameez* (long trousers with a long tunic top) is popular among the younger generation. In the big cities teenagers and young women wear jeans with tops or blouses. There are different types of *salwar kameez* and *sharee* to choose from, including cotton, silk, or georgette *sharees*, and designer *sharees*. Weaving the materials for these garments is an important activity. Most of the fabrics are locally produced. Some are very traditional and nationally

and internationally famous, such as the *jamdani sharee*, which is characterized by geometric or floral designs Although the term *jamdani* generally refers to *sharees*, there are *jamdani* scarves, *kurtas* (knee-length shirts), skirts, handkerchiefs, screens, and tablecloths as well. In the seventeenth century garments like the *sherwani* (a long, formal jacket for men) were made of *jamdani* fabric. Now the Bangladesh government is actively supporting the *jamdani* industry. After the war of liberation, a *jamdani* village was established near Dhaka to provide financial support to weavers. Some private businesses and NGOs also have *jamdani* projects and help the weavers with their trade and marketing. The most striking characteristic of *jamdani* work is its geometric design. The expert weavers do not need to draw the design on paper. They do it by instinct.

Among men, Western attire is more widely worn. Bangladeshi men sometimes wear a *Panjabi kurta* or a *fotua* (a short-sleeved version of the *kurta*) on religious and cultural occasions. In villages most men wear a *lungi* (sarong) as casual dress. In urban areas men wear shirts and trousers or suits on formal occasions. It is not considered proper to wear the *lungi* outside the house except by the farmers and low-income families.

Purdah, or the veil, is not compulsory in Bangladeshi society. Women are supposed to dress modestly. Some women choose to wear a *hijab* (covering their hair, head, and neck) or *burqah* (the head-to-toe veil). The *hijab* is fairly new and an imported custom for Bangladeshi Muslims. Previously women used to cover their heads with the end of their *sharee* or the *orna* (a kind of scarf worn with *salwar kameez*). But the *hijab* has become popular with some in Bangladesh as in Muslim societies all over the world.

There are certain colors for certain occasions. On Shaheed Dibas (Language Martyrs' Day) women wear a white *sharee* with a black border or black designs. Men wear a *Panjabi kurta* or *fotua* with the same color combination. On the first day of spring, women wear saffron-colored dresses. For the New Year the combination is white and red.

Bangladeshi women wear an ornamental dot on their forehead called a *tip* or *bindi*. Some people think this is a Hindu tradition, as it is the custom for married Hindu women to put a red spot on their forehead, and also at the parting of their hair, with vermilion. But in Muslim-dominated Bangladesh it is part of the general culture. Even in villages, small girls will put a *tip* on their foreheads when they are going to a fair, or if they are invited to someone else's house. They used to do it with kohl; now they can buy self-adhesive *tips* or *bindis* at the market. In dresses, dressing up, and doing their faces, most Bengali women follow the age-old Bengali traditions.

In the countryside people are more conservative, and if you are going to a village or small town, it is a good idea not to wear short dresses. Men can wear shorts.

VISITING BANGLADESHI HOMES

When visiting a Bangladeshi's home, it is customary to bring sweets or chocolates. Do not give alcohol or products containing non-*halal* meat to Muslims. Gifts should be offered with both hands. People are not punctual and you can arrive within half an hour of the stated time, but don't arrive too early—they may not be ready for you. You can call without giving notice if you have become close to someone or their family.

In some houses, you are expected to take your shoes off before entering. If you are unsure, ask your hosts whether they'd like you to do that. In urban homes, people have sofas in the sitting area and even in villages most Bangladeshi homes have chairs. They will not expect you to sit on the floor. They will offer you tea or coffee, and the beverage usually comes with snacks such as biscuits, different types of *pakoras* (a fried dough similar to fritters, sometimes made with vegetables), and homemade sweets. In villages, they will offer you *muri* (fluffed rice) with *gur* (jaggery), *batasha* (small round sweets made with jaggery), or *pitha* (local cakes made with rice flour).

If one is invited for a meal it is rude to turn the invitation down flatly. One should always use less direct language to suggest that it may be difficult such as "I

will try," "I will have to see," or "I would like to come, but I have another appointment."

Most Bengali people eat with their fingers, but it won't be taken amiss if you ask for cutlery. Out of politeness, you should wash your hands both before and after the meal as they do. Guests are generally served first. You will constantly be urged to take more food. Simply saying "I'm full" will be taken as a polite gesture and not be accepted at face value. It is therefore always best to pace yourself to allow for more helpings, but let your hosts understand firmly but politely when you can't manage any more. The left hand is considered unclean, so be careful to eat, pass dishes, and drink with the right hand only. Also do not take food from the bowl or the dishes the food is served in with the spoon or fork you are eating with. Bengalis are very particular about using cutlery already used by others—they call it "*jhuta*" or "*ento*" (which means "used by another person").

In modern households, all the family members and guests, men and women, eat together. In some cases, there may be some segregation. Women generally like to serve everyone else first and then eat. In rural areas meals are definitely segregated; women may not appear before you, or if they do it will only be to serve.

GOING OUT WITH FOREIGNERS

Dating foreigners is not a crime in Bangladesh, though it may cause exactly the same kind of problem as when the son or daughter of any family is dating and their parents do not like it. Society is traditional. Bangladeshi women are not promiscuous or sexually free, and respect must be shown. If you meet someone you would like to take out or be with, pause and try to understand their feelings. If you are sure that they'll agree to go out with you, ask them politely. If you are going to a restaurant or café, you (or whoever invites the other) should pay. As Bangladesh is a patriarchal society, the men normally pay. If you are in a group, then sometimes the women may offer to contribute to the bill.

Previously it was Bangladeshi men who had foreign fiancées or wives. Now the picture is changing, and many Bangladeshi women are marrying foreign men. In most cases their parents accept it, but they may try to convert the foreign spouse to their own religion, using some pressure. At one time even a mixed-faith marriage between two Bangladeshis encountered this problem, with one partner having to convert (usually to the Islamic faith) before there could be a marriage. But not anymore: a mixed-faith couple can now marry without a conversion, under the Special Marriage Act, 1872, and its amendments.

If a foreigner is married to a Bangladeshi national, he or she is entitled to a "No Visa Required" stamp in their passport, allowing them to enter the country freely or to stay as long as they want.

PRIVATE & FAMILY LIFE

WHO IS FAMILY?

Bangladeshi families are very close-knit. A family means not only immediate blood relations—father, mother, children—but also grandparents, uncles, aunts, and cousins. In towns they may live together under one roof. In rural areas, they may live in separate houses sharing a common courtyard. Bangladeshis keep in touch with their extended family, even distant relations. In Bengali there are special words for the different categories of uncle or aunt. Thus, a maternal uncle is called *Mama* and a paternal uncle is *Chacha*. The same goes for the aunts—they are called *Khala* or *Fufu* depending on whether they are maternal or paternal. Cousins are regarded as brothers and sisters. If Khaled is someone's uncle's son, he will be introduced as a brother. Sometimes outsiders cannot tell whether two girls are sisters or cousins. Not only first cousins, but second cousins are treated the same way. This extended family is usually involved in most major decisions and events concerning its members, and they look after one another.

In recent times, nuclear families have been growing in number among the urban population. Sometimes, the eldest member of the family will try to hold the extended family together, but after the death of that person family members separate into their own nuclear families, consisting of husband, wife, and children only. Even so, they will try to keep in touch with the others in the family. In villages, members of poor families, if they do not own land, may move away even while their parents are still alive. A widowed mother or widower father is usually made a part of the nuclear family. Sometimes people even keep their elderly uncle or aunt with them. In Bangladesh, retirement homes and nursing homes have not yet become a part of the social structure; just a few have been started of late. Families still feel ashamed to put their elderly relatives in these institutions. For the time being at least, they consider it their duty to look after elderly family members.

ELDERS

The traditional custom of respecting elders, whether they are a family member, an acquaintance, or just a neighbor, is still alive in Bangladesh. Elder members are respected by the younger generation and can command the rest of the family, too. In many cases the head of the family may not be the main earner but the family elder. Older people are considered wise. The young will listen to them politely, and never raise their voices or smoke in front of an elderly person.

Age dictates how people are addressed. As we have seen, people of the same age who know each other use first names. Otherwise Bangladeshis append a suffix to a person's name to denote respect and the level of closeness. Thus, for example, if the older person's name is Rahman he will be called Rahman *Bhai* (elder brother) or Rahman *Chacha* (uncle). In case of a woman named Shirin, she will be called Shirin *Apa* (elder sister) or Shirin *Khala* (aunt).

THE HOUSEHOLD

Family homes are different in urban and rural areas.

In cities, most families live in apartments these days. The traditional beautiful detached houses with gardens have gone, and in their places multistory apartment blocks are being built. Some poor people still live in shantytowns and slums. In rural areas, people live in detached houses, big or small depending on their circumstances. Houses with thatched roofs have also gone. Most now have tin roofs, with bamboo, earthen, or cement walls. Houses in villages normally have courtyards.

In urban areas, many women work outside the home for a living, but the home is still run by them. They have to handle practically all the household chores, like cooking, cleaning, and catering to the needs of the men in the house. In rural areas, women may not have any say in decision-making, although they are responsible for running the household.

Shopping for groceries, fish, or meat also differs in urban and rural areas. In the cities, many middle-class women do the day-to-day shopping that used to be done by male servants twenty or thirty years ago. These days there are supermarkets in every neighborhood frequented by women. This is almost a daily routine, as Bangladeshis like fresh food for every meal. In villages, though, men do the grocery shopping. Many households nowadays employ part-time domestic help or maids.

The main meal in both urban and rural areas is supper, as most people are out of the house during the day. It normally consists of boiled rice, vegetables, lentils, and fish, or occasionally meat.

KEEPING THE HOUSE IN ORDER

The responsibility for keeping the house in order mostly falls upon the woman of the family. Men provide for the family and take big decisions. But deciding what to buy from the market or what to cook, keeping in mind what everyone likes to eat or does not eat, is the woman's job. Buying the children's clothes is another responsibility. In most cases it is the woman who has to send the children off to school, supervise their homework, and decide when their playtimes should be.

Many women work outside the home these days and may have a share in decision-making, but this practice is not yet very widespread. Men still like to think of themselves as masters of the household. But this attitude is changing now that women are earning wages and their opinions are being taken into account.

WOMEN

Life expectancy, access to healthcare, and nutrition have improved for women in Bangladesh, and their mobility has also increased.

The status of women in Bangladesh has improved greatly in recent times but remains considerably inferior to that of men. Most women's lives remain centered on their traditional household roles. In rural areas, helped by NGO activities and becoming the main recipients of microcredit from the Grameen Bank (see p. 48), many women have improved their lot, but there is still a long way to go.

In the past, the economic contribution of women was also substantial but largely unacknowledged. Women in rural areas worked in the fields and were responsible for most of the post-harvest work, such

as husking, and for keeping livestock and poultry. Women in the cities relied on domestic and traditional jobs for income, but since the 1980s they have been increasingly working in manufacturing, especially in the garment industry. The growing numbers of clothing firms have given a boost to women from low-income groups. Currently one-third of the total workforce employed by the garment industry is female.

Women with education work in government offices, healthcare, and teaching. They have also stepped into more unconventional fields. There are women pilots, automobile engineers, police officers; and they are joining the ranks of the elite police Rapid Action Battalion, the army, navy, air force, and fire service. Women run a separate battalion in the police

service. There are female train drivers, too. There are even women mountaineers: two Bangladeshi women climbed Mount Everest in 2012. The person who is number one in the country in running "outsourcing" is a woman. Women hold top positions in the IT and banking sectors. Female scientists have won national awards. Women entrepreneurs are doing very well in Bangladesh. They are entering the legal profession in increasing numbers. Many NGOs are led by women. All this has happened since the Liberation War.

CHILDREN

Bangladeshi children are brought up differently according to their backgrounds. It is not the gap between the urban and rural populations that determines this, but their economic status. In cities there are children who are very poor and have to start working at a very early age. Some collect dry leaves from under trees (for use as fuel), scrap paper, and discarded bottles from the streets and sell them for a few *paisa* in order to supplement their parents' income. Some may not have a family and have to take care of themselves from an early age. In villages very poor children do not even have these options; they try to work for others. Many help their peasant fathers and brothers in the fields, or their mothers in their household chores.

In Bangladesh child labor is banned by law, but in reality many children have to start earning early. One common form of employment for them is working as domestic helpers. If they are lucky they are well treated, and some may have the opportunity of an education and future jobs. Not everyone is so lucky. There are primary schools in all areas, and education is free. The rate of enrollment is impressive, but the dropout rate is also high. In urban areas there are schools for the street children and child domestic helpers, but persuading them to attend school on a regular basis is a challenge for the social workers.

Children's upbringing is mainly the mother's duty. In the extended family this is sometimes shared by other family members, such as a grandmother. In conservative families boys get more attention than girls. They are given preference in education. They are fed better pieces of fish and other good food. But of late this attitude has been changing. Boys used to be looked upon as an asset, who would look after their elderly parents. But now in many families girls are equally capable of doing so. Though the old habitual patriarchal attitude still prevails, in many families today girls get the same treatment as their brothers and son-preference is decreasing. The mother is the person who is closest to children for most of their life, but what they should study or what kind of jobs they should seek are big decisions made by the father or the male elders of the family.

Children are treated with much love and affection in Bangladesh. They are pampered and disciplined at the same time. They are respectful toward their extended family members, elderly relatives, and teachers, and they obey them.

Many Bangladeshi children are obliged to live lives full of difficulties and hardship, but they are amazingly resilient. They manage to find fun in whatever they do, whether it is a game or collecting empty bottles on the streets.

EDUCATION

The education of their children is very important for most Bangladeshi parents. In urban areas most children go to school. In rural areas they go to school but the dropout rate is high, especially among girls. Parents have high aspirations for their children. Typically, whatever they could not be they want their children to achieve—to become doctors, engineers, and so on. Even the poor want to improve the situation of their children through education. The government has launched many programs and incentives to encourage poor parents to send their children to school.

Bangladesh conforms fully to its "Education for All" objectives. Article 17 of the Bangladesh Constitution stipulates that all children should be educated free of charge between the ages of six and eighteen years. The educational system is highly subsidized, and the government runs many schools at the primary, secondary, and higher secondary levels. It also subsidizes part of the

funding for many private schools, and supports more than fifteen state universities.

The three main educational systems in Bangladesh are:
• general education system,
• *madrasah* education system,
• technical–vocational education system.

Each of these three main systems is divided into five levels:
• primary level (classes 1–4),
• junior level (classes 5–8),
• secondary level (classes 9–10),
• higher secondary level (classes 11–12),
• tertiary level (college/university).

Tertiary education in Bangladesh takes place at thirty-four public, seventy-eight private, and three international universities. Students can choose to further their studies in chartered accountancy, engineering, information technology, agriculture, medicine, or business studies at a variety of universities and colleges.

Schools run by NGOs operate mainly in areas

not served either by the government or private schools, essentially to meet the educational needs of vulnerable groups in society. They usually follow an informal approach to suit the special needs of children from these groups. Today, however, some NGO schools are also operating in places where there are both private and government schools.

In the cities, students can choose to receive their education in English or Bengali. Most urban parents tend to choose English-medium schools for their children.

The school year is also different for the different education systems. In the general and *madrasah* education systems, the year starts in January and ends in December. For private English-medium schools following the British system, it starts in July and ends in June. School times also vary and classes may run in two shifts. In government schools, the morning shift is from 7:30 to 11:00 a.m. and the afternoon shift is from 11:30 a.m. to 4:30 p.m. In private schools, the morning shift runs from 7:30 a.m. to 1:30 p.m. and the afternoon shift from 2:30 to 5:30 p.m. There are many English-medium schools in urban areas.

The main school vacation is in summer. There are other, short vacations on different religious and social occasions.

THE CHANGING FAMILY
The country's social structure started to change after the Liberation War of 1971. Before then very few women worked in paid jobs. After the war, many families had lost their main breadwinner, and women had to leave the house and look for

employment. The famine of 1974 also played a role. This new situation changed society's attitudes toward women; but despite going out to work women still bear the main responsibility for caring for children and the elderly.

Arranged marriage, with the girl's consent, is still the norm and is a culturally accepted custom. After marriage the bride traditionally goes to live with her in-laws. But the number of young couples setting up home on their own, particularly in the urban areas, among garment workers and college students, is increasing.

There is a marked generation gap, with a strong Western influence evident in the younger generation. Some young people do not want to follow the values of their parents or the older generation. They are more interested in Facebook and cell phones and the Internet, and see themselves as part of the global village. There is also a gap between the urban and the rural populations, but this divide is becoming blurred.

There are increasing numbers of single parents in Bangladeshi society. Today society accepts them, which was not the case three or four decades ago. Women have become more independent. They have jobs and many of them raise their children on their own. As the scope of support services such as childcare facilities is still very limited in Bangladesh, they have to rely on their families or friends for the care of their children when they are at work. Many grandparents take on this responsibility.

The preference for sons, as we have seen, is weakening, and sons and daughters are treated as equals by younger parents.

chapter six

TIME OUT

Bangladeshis are very sociable. They think of leisure not as something separate, but as part of their lifestyle. They somehow find the time for it. There is a Bengali word, *adda*, which means people getting together and chatting for hours. *Adda* can take place during a work break, after work, or at holiday times. It doesn't need a specific place or time. It can happen anywhere. In villages, people gather in the marketplace to exchange information, talk about their problems or politics, and indulge in idle gossip. Someone who is educated will read the newspaper out aloud so that another ten can listen and know what's happening around the country or in the world. On a morning or evening stroll in the park, you'll see people stopping for a quick *adda*, whether it's just two people or a group.

Apart from *adda*, a favorite leisure activity is going to the cinema. In urban areas, theater has a following among the affluent classes, and there are occasional concerts and other cultural activities.

Sports are very popular. Cricket, in particular, is like a religion in Bangladesh. You can see boys from all backgrounds playing it in the fields, on the roadside, or wherever they can find the space. If they don't have a bat or wickets they'll happily improvise with a few sticks for the wickets or a bit of board or plank for the bat. Other popular games are football (soccer) and *kabaddi* (see page 120). Kite flying is a traditional pastime.

Eating out, spending time with family, visiting friends or relatives, or having the occasional picnic are some of the many other ways that Bangladeshis enjoy themselves.

BENGALI CUISINE

Bengali cuisine is hot, slightly spicy, and quite different from the North Indian cuisine that is popular in the West. The Bengali diet has more vegetables, cooked in many different ways, and uses various types of legumes. Fish is very popular; meat—whether goat (called mutton here), cow (beef), and chicken—is eaten only occasionally. Rice and fish are the staple diet, leading to the saying "*Machhey bhate Bangali*" ("Fish and rice make a Bengali").The Bengalis are also called "*bhojon rasik*," or connoisseurs of good food. Meat is considered a special treat when inviting guests.

There is a variety of distinctive sweetmeats made from milk products. These include:
Roshogolla Cottage cheese balls immersed in dense sugar syrup. *Rosh* means "sugary syrup" and *golla* means "round like a ball."

Shondesh Made using *chhana*, or cottage cheese, prepared by tossing the *chhana* lightly with sugar over low heat, then drying and
pressing it. It can be made in different shapes.
Chom chom Made with flour, cream, sugar, saffron, and lemon juice. It is normally oval-shaped.
Pantua Like *roshogolla*, but fried and dipped in syrup.
Rosomalai Small, marble-sized *roshogolla* submerged in sweet, creamy milk.
The makers of sweetmeats are quite inventive and are always experimenting with new dishes.

There are some very traditional sweets called *pitha*. These are a sort of cake made with rice flour. They are mostly sweet, but they can also be savory. *Pitha* are winter food and are part of the seasonal celebrations. In rural Bangladesh, at the festival of Nabanno, different types of *pitha* are made and villagers gather together to eat.

The Bengalis of Bangladesh share the same foods with Indian Bengalis, but there are some differences. In Bangladesh there is a dish called *bharta*, which is very popular and is part of the daily meal. It consists mainly of mashed vegetables such as potato, eggplant, and beans, mixed with mustard oil, chopped onion, green chili, and coriander leaves. *Bharta* can be made with any vegetables. It can also be made with fish or meat. There could easily be a hundred different types of *bharta*. Then there are different types of *shaak* (spinach, or greens). Another favorite dish is *khichuri*, rice and lentils cooked together, which is associated with rain. During the rainy seasons, Bengalis love to have *khichuri* with fried fish. And of course, *biriyani* and *kababs* are also popular.

Bengal's vast repertoire of fish-based dishes

includes many different *ilish* preparations. *Ilish,* or *hilsa,* is the most popular fish among Bengalis. It can reach 24 inches (60 cm) long, but usually measures around 15 inches (38 cm). Its metallic-

looking silver body is covered in medium-sized scales and it has many bones. *Ilish* can be called the country's signature dish. Bangladeshis take pride in it, and they love it. There are people who would not

tire of eating this fish every day of the year.

The favorite drink in Bangladesh is tea, both with milk and black, though some people prefer coffee. In summer, people like drinking *shorbot*, a drink

made of water, freshly squeezed lemon, and sugar. It can be mixed with syrups that are available in the market, such as rose syrup, lime syrup, and so on. Alcohol is prohibited in Bangladesh as it is a predominantly Muslim country, but foreign passport holders can buy alcohol.

Eating Together
Almost everyone enjoys eating together, whether it is eating out or at home. Without any particular reason Bangladeshis may invite someone, or a group of people, to dine with them. Families try to have at least one meal together every day, usually in the evening. Whatever anyone is doing, they will have to be at the table for that meal. In villages, they eat sitting on mats spread on the floor, sometimes around the earthen cooker, or *chula*. Normally the *chula* is placed outside, in a corner of the courtyard. While having a meal together people discuss the day's work or what they have heard or seen outside the house. They may talk politics, too. Elder members of the family tell stories of yesteryear. They may also discuss serious family problems. Eating together gives everybody the opportunity to catch up with one another.

Because the left hand is considered unclean, Bengalis eat with the right hand only. If passing a dish around with the left hand, some people will touch its bottom or side with the back of their right hand. Others may say "Sorry for left hand."

DINING OUT
The practice of dining out is increasing among urban Bangladeshis. Not only the elite, but also

low-income earners go out with their families to restaurants or small eateries. People will eat out on special occasions—birthdays, marriage anniversaries, and so on—and will book in advance for an important celebration.

Restaurants in the big cities range across a large spectrum. Chinese food is an all-time favorite. You can also find Thai, Korean, Afghan, Italian, Lebanese, and different kinds of fast-food joints, not to mention international fast-food chains such as KFC, Pizza Hut, and Nando's. There are many good restaurants serving traditional Bengali dishes, not all of which are expensive. If a restaurant is crowded, you can generally assume that it is good. Otherwise, you can ask people you know to recommend one.

TIPPING

In some restaurants you will have to wait to be seated, in others you can take a seat where you like. Waiters will come with the menu and take the order. Don't forget to leave a tip when they bring the bill at the end, even if a service charge has been included. The person serving you may not get anything if you include your tip in the bill. The unofficial rule is to pay 10 percent, but many pay less than that. Tipping is expected for any service provided, by porters at the stations, rickshaw wallas, or the staff at the hotel where you are staying. There is no rule about how much you should pay; a reasonable amount, say 100 Taka (US $1.29), will make them happy.

The old part of Dhaka takes pride in its *Moghlai*, or Mughal, cuisine—typically North Indian dishes such as *kabab*, *biriyani*, or *morog* (chicken) *pulao*. Restaurants here offer Bangladeshi versions of classic North Indian food. There are similar establishments in other parts of the city as well. Different kinds of *kabab* are very popular and are served in many restaurants. You can even find "continental" (that is, European) food in the capital. Many clubs serve good food, but these are for members only, who are drawn from the elite.

There are no public bars selling alcohol. Those who want to drink do so at home or in clubs. Cafés and snack bars offering tea, coffee, soft drinks, snacks, and light food, such as sandwiches or pizzas, are very popular with the young wishing to hang out for *adda*.

CULTURAL ACTIVITIES
There are cultural events for almost every occasion. The birth and death anniversaries of the poets

Rabindranath Tagore and Nazrul Islam are celebrated in a big way all over the country, with public performances of their songs and poems, and seminars and discussions. Language Martyr's Day, Bengali New Year, the spring festival, and Nabanno, the harvest festival, are also celebrated with cultural programs.

Bangladeshi culture has marked differences from the neighboring regions. It has evolved over centuries and encompasses the country's diverse social groups and the influences of its different religions. This is manifest in all its forms: music, dance and drama; arts and crafts; folklore and folktales; languages and literature.

Music and Dance

The music and dance styles of Bangladesh can be divided into three categories: classical, folk, and modern. The classical style has been influenced by the major classical forms of the Indian subcontinent. Bharata Natyam, for example, is a dance form based on the art of ancient temple dancers called *Devadasis*, and is known for its grace and statuesque poses. The dance known as Kathak traces its origins to the nomadic bards of ancient northern India known as *kathakars*, or storytellers. The dancers tell a story through their poses. This form is a mixture of temple and ritual dances and contains some

Persian and central Asian influences, imported
by the royal courts of the Mughal era.

Bangladeshi folk and tribal music and dance is
indigenous and deeply rooted. However, several
tribal dances from across northeastern India, such
as the Manipuri, Chakma, and Santal dances, are
also widely popular.

The unique Bangladeshi folk song tradition is
rooted in a mix of spirituality, mysticism, and
devotion. The main forms of folk music include
Bhatiali (boat songs sung by Bangladeshi river
boatmen); Baul (mystical songs of the wandering
Bauls, through which they express their philosophy
and views on life); Murshidi (devotional songs that
praise *murshids*, who are spiritual gurus, which
evolved and flourished mainly through Sufism);
and Bhawaiya (folk songs from northern Bengal,
believed to have originated in Rangpur and Cooch
Bihar in India; these are basically love songs,
though there may also be a spiritual theme). The
Bangladeshi folk song tradition has been enriched
by lyricists such as Hason Raja, Kangal Haridas,

Romesh Sheel, Abbas Uddin, and countless anonymous writers.

The songs of the remarkable poets Rabindranath Tagore and Nazrul Islam form a great part of the precious cultural heritage of Bangladesh.

In recent times, Western influence has given rise to several quality rock bands playing in a style popularly known as Band Music, particularly in urban centers. Sometimes this is a mixture of folk and rock.

Typical musical instruments used in Bangladesh, some of them indigenous in origin, are the bamboo flute (*banshi*), drums (*dhol*), the

single-stringed *ektara*, a two-stringed instrument called the *dotara*, and the *mandira*, a pair of small metal bowls struck together to make a bell-like sound for rhythmic effect. All are important in the culture of Bangladesh. Today several Western musical instruments—drums, keyboard, violin, guitar, and so on—are also used, sometimes alongside traditional instruments.

Theater
Traditionally, the open-air *jatra* was very popular in towns and villages (see page 83). Today tastes have changed, however, and people are more likely to go to the movies. Since liberation, on the other hand,

the theater in Bangladesh has developed to a remarkable standard. There are many amateur dramatic groups in the cities, commonly called Group Theatre. At one time, there were annual performances of plays in many corporate offices. Nowadays the Group Theatre troupes are popular, offering a mixture of Western and traditional plays. There are theater festivals, too.

Film
There has been a film industry in the eastern part of Bengal since the late 1920s. It developed further after the Liberation War and went on to produce films with outrageous storylines, full of sex and violence to draw the audiences. But today, helped by government incentives, a new generation of filmmakers is producing films that are acclaimed internationally, such as *Matir Moina* (*The Clay Bird*) and *Khelaghor* (*Doll House*). Every year good documentaries and short films are also made. With the opening of multiplex cinemas in Bangladesh, more people are gaining access to good films.

Theater and Film Studies are included in the curriculum at some universities. Television programs, television dramas of various kinds, and serials are widely popular.

Art
For contemporary and classical Bangladeshi fine art there are many galleries worth visiting in Dhaka. These include the Shilpakala Academy Art Gallery, the National Museum Gallery, the Osmany Memorial Hall Gallery, the Bengal Gallery of Fine Arts, the Dhaka Art Centre, Shilparag, Chitrak, Aerial, and Gallery Kaya.

Bangladeshis love color and pattern. They paint the pottery they use in daily life, and some tribal peoples paint decorative designs on the walls of their homes. At weddings and on special occasions they create *alponas*—motif-based floor paintings. This is a traditional art form in which designs made with colored powders (made from dried leaves, charcoal, or burnt earth) mixed in a thick paste of rice flour and water are applied to the floor or ground, either by hand or using cotton.

On the eve of Shaheed Dibas (Language Martyr's Day), students of the Faculty of Fine Arts at Dhaka University paint an *alpona* on the road along the route of the procession to the Shaheed Minar. They also do this at Bengali New Year. On April 14, 2014, the eve of the Bengali year 1421, ex-students and students of the Faculty, and even some bystanders, painted the largest *alpona* in the world on Manik Miah Avenue, in front of the Shongshod Bhavan (Parliament House). It covered an area of 326,000 square feet (30,286 sq. m).

SPORTS AND GAMES

Sports are an essential part of Bangladeshi culture. *Kabaddi*, or *Hadudu*, an outdoor wrestling game played by two teams of twelve players, is the national sport of Bangladesh. However, cricket and football (soccer) are by far the most popular games. Cricket, as we have seen, is almost like a religion for many Bangladeshis. Next is football. The national cricket team first participated in World Cup tournaments in 1999. In 2011, Bangladesh successfully co-hosted the ICC Cricket World Cup tournament with India and Sri Lanka.

Other popular sports are field hockey, tennis, badminton, handball, basketball, volleyball, golf, shooting, angling, carom billiards, and chess.

Traditional sports like *kabaddi*, *boli khela* (wrestling), and *lathi khela* (stick fighting) are mostly played in the rural areas, while foreign sports such as cricket, football, hockey, volleyball, handball, golf, and badminton are more popular in the cities. The National Sports Council (NSC) is the governing body that controls all the sports federations and councils in the country and is responsible to the Ministry of Youth and Sports. There are a total of forty-two different sports federations affiliated with the NSC. The Bangladesh Games is the largest domestic multisport tournament in the country, in which athletes and sports teams from all the districts participate.

Women are also taking an interest in sports and joining in enthusiastically, and games are no longer an exclusively male affair. Bangladesh is trying to raise its profile in the global sports arena.

SHOPPING FOR PLEASURE

Today shopping is becoming a form of leisure across the classes. There are malls in every city and their numbers are growing. Famous brand names are part of the scene, but the most striking products reflect the Bangladeshi tradition in handicrafts. While the muslin of ancient Dhaka may have gone into history, there are traditional Jamdani *sharees*, *nakshi kantha* (embroidered quilts), and other products that are still very popular and make excellent gifts and souvenirs. Embroidered clothes are also popular. Items such as contemporary paintings, small wood carvings, *shital pati* (mats made with bamboo and cane to give a cooling effect), bamboo decorative pieces, cane and conch shell

products, cotton, silk, gold, silver, jute, reed, brassware, traditional dolls, and leather goods are sought after by lovers of arts and crafts. In addition, Bangladesh is famous for its lustrous pink pearls.

Apart from the malls, there are markets and small boutiques where you can get everything from clothing to pottery. The boutiques normally have fixed prices, but in markets you are expected to bargain. Whatever the asking price, you should go down to a half or a third and you can settle somewhere in the middle. Sometimes, if you walk away, the merchant will call you back and agree to accept the sum you offered. Bargaining is cheerful, with no hard feelings.

You can use credit or debit cards in many shops. Some may inform you that if paying by card you'll pay more, or that if you pay by cash you will get a discount. When shopping in Bangladesh, you will be given your goods in a paper or cloth bag, as plastic bags are banned.

SIGHTSEEING

Bangladesh has it all—heritage sites; archaeological sites; scenic landscapes crisscrossed by rivers; wildlife; forests; tribal cultures; historical mosques, temples, Buddhist relics and monuments; hill resorts; areas of natural beauty; and a rich cultural diversity. The land of Bengal has attracted tourists from ancient times, and you will be made welcome everywhere you go. The Bangladesh Parjatan (Tourism) Corporation is responsible for the tourist infrastructure. Recently the government adopted a plan to highlight the country's attractions styled *Rupamoy Bangladesh* (Beautiful Bangladesh). There are many private tour operators, resorts, and other facilities. Traveling is not difficult. You can reach many places by air; other destinations are served by buses and trains, and intercity road conditions are very good.

In Dhaka

The capital city, Dhaka, is located on the banks of the Buriganga River. It was founded and made the provincial Mughal capital in 1608, a status it enjoyed until 1717. In Dhaka city there is a lot to see, including the magnificent Ahsan Manzil, former residence of the Nawabs, the Lalbagh Fort, the Imambara (house of the *imam*) Husaini Dalan of the Shia Muslims, the Shaheed Minar national monument, the National Museum, and the Muktijuddho Jadughar (Liberation War Museum). Near Dhaka is the monument called Savar Smriti Soudha, the memorial for the martyrs of the 1971 Liberation War.

The **Lalbagh Fort**, or Fort Aurangabad, was constructed by the third son of the Mughal emperor Aurangzeb and Viceroy of Bengal, Prince Muhammad Azam, in 1678, and by his successor, Shaista Khan. The decorative walls and gates, a fine masonry tank, the audience hall, mosque, and the

tomb of Pari Bibi are important attractions inside the fort.

The palatial **Bara Katra**, situated on the north bank of the Buriganga River, was built as a residence in 1644 by Abdul Qasim, Diwan of Shah Shuja. (A *katara*, or *katra*, was a colonnaded building built around a courtyard. An arched veranda surrounded the courtyard, behind which were the rooms.) A smaller version, the **Chhota Katra**, about 200 yards (183 m) east of the Bara Katra, was built in 1663 by Shaista Khan. These two Katras are among the important examples of Mughal architecture in the capital. There are a few more forts near Dhaka city.

The **Ahsan Manzil** was the Nawab's official residence, and is situated on the bank of the Buriganga. The palace was originally built in 1872 by Nawab Abdul Ghani and is now a museum.

The **Baldah Garden** is the creation of Narendra Narayan Roy, landlord of the Baldah Estate. Established in 1904 in the old part of the city, the 3.5-acre (1.4-ha) garden has a large collection of indigenous and exotic plants. It is managed by the Forestry Department as part of the National Botanical Garden. The **National Botanical Garden** at Mirpur, near Dhaka Zoo, is spread over 205 acres (about 83 ha) of land.

Outside Dhaka

Many of Bangladesh's major towns are well worth visiting. **Chittagong**, the second-largest city of Bangladesh and an important seaport, has a picturesque hinterland of large hill-forests and lakes. Its many attractive places of interest include the shrine of Bayajid Boshtomi, a Second World War cemetery, Foy's Lake, the Ethnological Museum, Patenga Beach, and Sitakunda, a holy place for Hindus. Not far from Chittagong city are the man-made lakes of Rangamati and Kaptai.

Sonargaon, an old capital of Bengal about 16.15 miles (26 km) east of Dhaka, is home to a Folk Art Museum.

Sylhet town, 217 miles (350 km) from Dhaka, is famous for its natural setting, which includes the Khasi-Jaintia hills. The district is also famous for its tea gardens. For Muslims Sylhet is a holy city where the shrines of the saints Shah Jalal, Shah Paran, and others are located. There is a place where Shree Chaitanya, the late fifteenth-century founder of the Vaishnava cult, spent some years of his youth, and many Hindus gather there for religious observances.

In the northwestern town of **Rajshahi**, the Bara Kuthi, built by the Dutch East India Company on the bank of the Padma River, and the Varendra Research Museum are attractions for lovers of history and antiquity. A fine silk is produced in Rajshahi and tourists can visit the Bangladesh Sericulture Board to see how it is made. The Islamic monuments of medieval Gour are 54.7 miles (88 km) from Rajshahi town. These are scattered over an area of more than 2.3 square miles (6 sq. km).

Near the northern town of **Dinajpur**, Kantanagar Temple is an eighteenth-century terracotta structure. This *nava-ratna* or "nine-spired" Hindu temple was damaged by an earthquake in 1897 and lost the original nine spires at its corners. Even so, it exhibits the exuberance of terracotta art at its best.

For travelers looking for natural beauty, there is no shortage of places to visit. Some of these, such as the long beach at Cox's Bazar and the great mangrove forests of the Sundarbans, have already been mentioned (see pages 15–16). Tours of the Sundarbans, home to the exotic breathing mangrove roots and many other trees, plants, birds, and wild animals, are arranged by the Parjatan Corporation and by many private operators.

There are good resorts in remote scenic places such as the Chittagong Hill Tracts and the northeastern division of Sylhet. Here are some other areas of outstanding natural beauty:

The National Park at Bhawal, 24.84 miles (40 km) north of Dhaka, has a 16,000-acre (6,475-ha) recreational forest. The main flora is the lofty *garja* (Assam *sal*) and the fauna include small bears, monkeys, porcupines, foxes, pythons, lizards, and many species of birds.

Hill districts with perennial forests, such as Khagrachhari and Bandarban, are home to the country's colorful tribal life and culture, and attractive handicrafts. On your way to Kaptai along the Chittagong Road lies the ancient Buddhist temple of Chit Morong with its beautiful statues.

Among the large bodies of water and wetland ecosystems in Sylhet are Tanguar Haor, Ratargul swamp forest, and the Madhabkunda waterfall.

Near Cox's Bazar, Himchhari is a picnic spot with a beautiful spring. You can also visit Teknaf, the southernmost tip of Bangladesh, the Buddhist temple at Ramu, and the nearby islands of St

Martin's, Sonadia, Kutubdia, and Moheshkhali.

There is a panoramic beach in the southern district of Patuakhali, about 199 miles (320 km) south of Dhaka, called Kuakata. The sandy beach is 11 miles (18 km) long and 1.87 miles (3 km) wide. Many Hindus and Buddhists come here during religious festivals to bathe in Kuakata's waters, which they believe to be holy.

There are several old Buddhist temples at Keranipara, Misripara, and Amkholapara.

ARCHAEOLOGICAL SITES
There are three major archaeological sites in the country, famous for their sculptures in bronze, stone, and terracotta, their gold and silver coins, their ceramics, and their terracotta plaques.

Mahasthangarh
The oldest archaeological site in Bangladesh, Mahasthangarh dates back to 700 BCE and was the pre–Vedic city of Pundranagar, or Pundravardanapura. It is located on the bank of the Karotoya River in the northwestern Rajshai division; the nearest town is Bogra. It was a fortified ancient

city, and contains around thirty-six mounds of various sizes. Fragments of stone tablets have been discovered there, one of which has six lines of Brahmi script dating from the second or third century BCE, making it the earliest written document of Bengal. One of the sites has been identified as the grand monastery. The Chinese Buddhist monk and traveler Hiuen-Tsang (Xuan Zang) visited this site in the seventh century CE. Many artifacts found in Mahasthangarh are preserved in museums around the world, including the Bangladesh National Museum, the Indian Museum, the British Museum, and the Victoria and Albert Museum in London.

Paharpur

The spectacular Sompur (Somapura) Mahavihara in Paharpur, in the northern district of Naogaon, is one of the most famous Buddhist *viharas* (monasteries) in the Indian subcontinent, and one of the most important archaeological sites in Bangladesh.

Excavations, and the finding of clay seals with the inscription *Shri-Somapure-Shri-Dharmapaladeva-Mahavihariyarya-bhiksu-sangghasya*, identify it as being built by Dharmapala (c. 781–821), the second king of the Pala dynasty. Another inscription, of Vipulashrimitra, from the university of Nalanda in the Indian state of Bihar, records that the monastery city was destroyed by fire during a conquest by the Vanga army in the eleventh century, which also killed his ancestor Karunashrimitra. About a century after this, Vipulashrimitra renovated the monastery and built a temple dedicated to Tara, savior of those trapped in the cycle of *samsara* (reincarnation). Many Tibetan monks visited the Somapura between the ninth and twelfth centuries.

The excavations have revealed a 72-foot (22-m) shrine with an impressive courtyard and several *mandaps* (covered structures with pillars, often used for Hindu weddings and *pujas*) and terracotta panels depicting both Buddhist and Brahminical deities.

Paharpur was designated a UNESCO World Heritage Site in 1985.

Mainamoti and Shalbon Viharas

These Buddhist sites are set in a range of low hills in Comilla district, about 62 miles (100 km) southeast of Dhaka. The famous Shalbon Vihar, in the middle of the Lalmai–Mainamoti range, was established in the eighth century by King Buddhadev. It consists of 115 cells, built around a spacious courtyard with a temple in the center. This area was also visited by Hiuen-Tsang in the seventh century.

Kotila Mura, situated on a flattened hillock about 3 miles (5 km) north of Shalbon Vihara, has three stupas (dome-shaped Buddhist shrines) side by side, representing the Buddhist "Trinity," or the "Three Jewels"—the Buddha, Dharma, and Sangha. Charpatra Mura is an isolated small oblong shrine about 1.5 miles (2.5 km) to the northwest.

The scenes on the Paharpur and Mainamoti terracotta plaques depict Buddhist and Brahminical themes, folk tales, and the daily life of ancient Bengal.

chapter seven

TRAVEL, HEALTH, & SAFETY

Getting around in Bangladesh is generally enjoyable. The country has a reasonably good transportation infrastructure, with good roads to and within almost all the main districts, and even connecting the villages with one another. You can travel to most places by train, and to some destinations by plane or boat. Most intercity journeys are pleasant trips. There are roadside service areas with drinks, food, and toilets. In the cities, apart from the usual urban transportation, it is possible to rent cars quite cheaply, with or without a driver.

There is access to basic healthcare almost everywhere. In small places such as villages there may not be hospitals, but you will find doctors, medical centers, and the like. Bangladesh adopted a policy in the 1980s that controls and regulates the production, distribution, sale, and use of drugs. However, you will find all the medications you are likely to need in pharmacies. You have to be careful, though, about what and where you eat and drink.

Bangladesh is a generally safe country, but be aware that there is petty crime. Keep your valuables safe with you. Most people are friendly and helpful, sometimes intrusively so. But their intentions are good. If you are friendly toward them, they will look after you.

VISAS AND OTHER DOCUMENTS
Citizens of most countries require valid visas to enter Bangladesh. These can be obtained from the Bangladesh High Commission or Embassy in each country. The types and categories of visas differ according to the purpose of the visit, length of stay, and any bilateral arrangements.

When applying for a visa you have to submit certain documents together with the visa application form, depending upon the purpose of the visit. For example, for a tourist visa you need a travel itinerary and air ticket reservation; for a business visa you have to show a letter of invitation from a Bangladeshi business organization or establishment or a letter to the visa officer from a local business organization, clearly stating the purpose of your visit. Visa fees are determined on the basis of reciprocity with the country of the foreign applicant.

Nationals of some countries are exempt from all visa requirements, while nationals of others can be granted visas on arrival.

ENTRY POINTS AND ARRIVALS
The main entry point is the international airport at Dhaka. There are land crossings from India. There are frequent trains and buses from the Indian city of Kolkata. Many major airlines fly to Dhaka from most parts of the world. The Bangladeshi national carrier, Bangladesh Biman, also operates international flights.

A foreigner arriving in Bangladesh will need to fill out a landing card. The immigration check is routine, and is generally fairly quick. Visitors do not have to report anywhere or register with anyone, unless this is stipulated in the visa.

No one will demand bribes from you at the airport; if they do, you can report it to the authorities immediately.

INTERCITY TRAVEL
Rail

Rail services connect all parts of the country, apart from the district of Barisal. Barisal city, which is one of the major river ports, is served by bus. The railway network dates from the British period and not all the lines are in good condition. The train service from Dhaka to the second largest city, Chittagong, is very good. Conditions vary on intercity and local trains, and there are different classes of coach. These are AC (air-conditioned) first class; non–First Class; AC chair car (with individual seats, as opposed to shared cushioned benches) and non AC chair car; and sleepers. Chair cars are available only on some trains. Food is available in the pantry car. The lavatories on board may be both squatting and commode systems, depending on the class and route. They may not be very clean and there may not be any toilet paper, so it is a good idea to carry some with you. (People in Bangladesh use water to clean themselves after using the toilet.)

Book tickets well in advance or it may be difficult to get the date or class you want. During festive seasons such as Eid or Puja, when most people go to their hometowns and villages to be with their families, more trains are scheduled, but it is still difficult to get tickets. In chair cars Bengali songs or instrumental music is usually piped into the carriages. There are no steam trains in Bangladesh, only diesel locomotives.

Bus

After trains, buses are the most popular form of transport, and the bus network covers most destinations. As road conditions have improved, people today can even reach their villages by bus, instead of undertaking the last part of their journey by bullock cart. There are very comfortable luxury AC coaches, operating both day and nighttime services. You can book your seat in advance. They play music, which is a mixed blessing as you cannot control the volume. The best thing is to carry earplugs or headphones with your own source of music. The buses stop at roadside services where you can buy food and beverages. The service areas will have toilets, but the facilities vary in cleanliness and, again, there will probably be no toilet paper. In some areas, road signs and names of the places are in both Bengali and English.

At most river crossings there are bridges, but at others there are large ferries that can hold cars, buses, and trucks. A ferry crossing may take a couple of hours, but you can enjoy the fresh air and surrounding activity. You may even befriend a fellow traveler. These ferries have two or three decks, with seating arrangements upstairs where you can rest and enjoy the scenery. You can buy food and beverages from an onboard café and there will be roaming vendors selling peanuts, fruits, and other snacks. Some ferries have toilets, too. It is a good idea to get off the bus before it drives aboard.

On highways the upper speed limit is 96 mph (155 kmph) for light vehicles and 34 mph (55 kmph) for heavy vehicles. In towns it is 34 mph (55 kmph) for cars and 15.5 mph (25 kmph) for public transport.

By Air
There are eight domestic airports and you can fly to cities such as Chittagong, Rajshahi, Jessore, Sylhet, and Cox's Bazar. These are all short trips, but tickets can be quite expensive. Apart from the national flag carrier, Bangladesh Biman, there are flights by private airlines such as Novo Air, Regent Airways, and United Airways (BD) Ltd.

By Water
Bangladesh is a country of rivers and the water transportation system is highly organized and relatively cheap. There are many large motor launches with two or three decks run by both private and state-owned companies. The food on these boats is delicious, although some people say that it tastes better because the fresh river breeze gives you

an appetite. There are also a few old-time paddle steamers traveling between Dhaka and Khulna, and on sightseeing trips in the Sundarbans.

You have to book tickets well in advance for the bigger boats and for longer journeys. Water travel is a relaxing and rewarding experience. Watching the villages, markets, and corn and mustard fields as you glide by, you can get a feel for the timeless culture and way of life of Bangladesh.

GETTING AROUND TOWN
Rickshaw

Bangladesh is famous for its many, very colorful tricycle rickshaws, pedaled by *rickshaw-wallas* (rickshaw pullers) with usually two passengers sitting at the back, sometimes three. They have a retractable hood, which can be unfolded to protect the passengers from too much sun or rain. Almost all the cities and even some villages have cycle rickshaws. They are very different from the rickshaws of the Indian state of West Bengal. Rickshaws in Bangladesh are famous for their decorative art, which adds a splash of color to the streets. This rickshaw art features film stars, state leaders like Sheikh Mujibur Rahman with former Indian Prime Minister Indira Gandhi, airplanes, boats, launches, trains, flowers, birds, tigers, and other animals. Sometimes the proportions are not right—the size of the plane or ship and the humans

may be the same—but undoubtedly this folk art is part of the culture of Bangladesh.

Travel by rickshaw is the cheapest option. Rickshaws do not create any pollution, but they are no longer allowed on major roads in the cities, and are restricted to certain smaller roads only. They are a favorite with foreign visitors. There are some motorized rickshaws, but they are not licensed and are dangerous in crowded roads because it is difficult to control the speed.

Auto Rickshaw, or CNG
There are very few taxis in Bangladesh, despite various initiatives by government and private companies to promote them. There are, however, many auto rickshaws or three-wheelers (three-wheeled cabs with a motorcycle engine), known as CNGs as they are run by compressed natural gas. They will take you from door to door. Usually three people can travel in a CNG, but sometimes four can squeeze in. Passengers are protected by an iron net that only opens on one side.

Bus

City buses, run by both government and private
companies, are used mostly by the less well-off.
Some buses are modern, others not. There used to
be double-decker buses in Dhaka, but you only see
a few these days. The buses are crowded, not very
comfortable, and in summer, smelly. There are
separate Ladies' Seats at the front of all buses. After
those seats fill up, women can sit anywhere. In
Dhaka there are some luxury AC buses, too. On
some routes you can buy tickets before boarding,
and on others you have to buy them on board from
a conductor, who is sometimes called a "helper."

Hired Car

Car hire with a driver is not very expensive. Apart
from the international company Hertz, there are
many local car-hire companies. When hiring from
local companies, it is advisable to ask a Bangladeshi
which companies are good and reliable. Usually you
have to hire a car for a certain number of hours. If
you hire a car for a whole day, you should also give

the driver money for his lunch—100 Taka (US \$1.29 is about right.

In Bangladesh driving is on the left side of the road. Roads are well maintained. Traffic rules exist, but not everybody observes them. Red lights are sometimes taken as suggestions only. Speed limits within the city are from 12.43 to 24.9 mph (20 to 40 kmph), but you can hardly reach those speeds as there are terrible traffic jams in Dhaka city. If you have to travel during the rush hours, always allow plenty of extra time for your journey. Rush hours vary with office and school times. The main rush hours are from 7:00 to 9:00 a.m. and 5:00 to 7:00 p.m., but, as most schools finish in the afternoon, there is another rush hour from 1:00 to 3:00 p.m.

When you arrive in Dhaka and see all the cars yo might well expect there to be high levels of pollution but because many cars have been converted from petrol to compressed natural gas the pollution rate i

not as bad as you might thin

There are also, of course, those forms of transportation that are part of the traditiona culture. In rural areas bulloc carts, buffalo carts, and horse drawn carts are commonly used. Bicycles are widely used both in rural and urban areas.

WHERE TO STAY
In Dhaka there are a few five-star hotels as well as a number of middle-range hotels. There are also good hotels in other big cities, such as Chittagong. Most

places outside Dhaka today have hotels of differing standards. These include rest houses, motels, eco-resorts, NGO guest houses, and expensive resorts. The hotel situation has improved considerably in the past few years. If you are working with the government, you can stay at one of their guest houses or circuit houses. Again, find out by word of mouth which ones are good: ask someone you know. You can find their contact details on the Internet, and the Bangladesh Parjatan Corporation may also be able to help with accommodation.

HEALTH

Before going to Bangladesh you will need to have some vaccinations, depending on where you'll be staying and for how long. Your GP is the best person to approach about this, four to eight weeks before departure.

The provision of healthcare is generally good in Bangladesh. There are good hospitals, clinics, and nursing homes in the cities, but you have to pay for everything. There is no National Health Service or medical insurance system. There are good doctors, but you have to know about them. If you are in need, ask your host or another local person. There are doctors and healthcare centers in the villages too. Should you fall ill and be treated, and want to file a claim on your travel or health insurance, ask the hospital or doctors to give you a certificate specifying the treatment you've received.

You need to be aware of the weather in Bangladesh. If you go in summer, it will be hot and humid. Be careful when you go out, and use sun-protection lotions or creams. Winter, on the other hand, is mild and pleasant. Also be careful about what you eat and drink, because food spoils quickly in the heat and because of waterborne diseases. The best thing is to drink bottled water or boiled water. When eating out, choose food that is freshly cooked. Try to avoid salads as you do not know what water was used to wash them. Buying ready-to-eat sandwiches is also not very safe.

If you experience symptoms such as vomiting or an upset stomach, you can buy Oral Rehydration Solution (ORS), which is very good, or rice saline. These can be bought in almost all pharmacies.

Sanitation is good in the cities, less so in small places, unless you are staying in a good resort. When traveling, it is difficult to find good and clean toilets. Roadside service areas may have fairly clean facilities both squatting and Western style, with flush and water. But there will be no toilet paper, and it's advisable to carry some with you.

The numbers of mosquitoes are increasing with the rise in human population, and mosquito bites can cause infections such as dengue fever. It is strongly recommended to take mosquito repellent with you. Many people use mosquito nets around their beds, but in some places they only use repellent spray and do without a net. There are fewer mosquitoes in the summer before the monsoon season; their numbers increase in winter.

SAFETY

Bangladesh is generally a safe country. The only time it is not safe is when there is political unrest. Pay close attention to your personal security at all times and keep an eye on the media for news about possible safety or security risks. *Hartals*, or strikes, can involve the shutdown of all activities, particularly in urban areas. There are periodic blockades of rail, road, and river transport networks by political groups, which may involve disruption of movement around the country. Check before you travel anywhere in Bangladesh during these times.

Foreigners are easy targets for theft, so be mindful of pickpockets. Take the usual precautions such as keeping your money and bank cards hidden, and if you have a camera or handbag, hold it tight and keep an eye on it in crowded areas. Big hotels have safes or lockers where you can keep your valuables. You don't need to carry your passport every time you go out; you can leave it with the hotel.

Don't go to remote and isolated areas after dark, especially if you are not accompanied by a local acquaintance. In the evening, do not trust any stranger who volunteers to help you. Though there is generally no danger for women travelers, it is better to err on the safe side. Try to go out with a friend or acquaintance, or in a group. In the event of theft or an accident, the police are very helpful, especially to foreigners. They will not ask you for a bribe.

You can go freely anywhere in Bangladesh except the Chittagong Hill Tracts (CHT). The vast forests and hilly areas bordering northeast India may harbor Indian separatist insurgents (there have been kidnappings of foreigners for ransom on both sides of the border) and you will need permission from the army to go there, which is generally granted. All people have to report to the army before entering the CHT. Foreigners are advised to inform the military and civil authorities prior to their visit.

chapter eight

BUSINESS BRIEFING

THE BUSINESS CLIMATE

Bangladeshis today are an enterprising people.
Long ago, in the 1930s, '40s, or '50s, most young
people used to follow in their fathers' footsteps and
join the professions or the offices where they

worked. Very few considered
going it alone in business,
having neither the aptitude
nor the skills for it. But the
situation has changed. Since
1971, the younger generation
has embraced the business
ethos and is doing rather well.
There is a large number of
young entrepreneurs who are
driving the economy. Despite the handicaps of
political instability and an inefficient bureaucracy,
business is flourishing, and in the last ten years
exports have shot up from US $5 billion to US $25
billion a year, creating an attractive environment
for foreign investors. Small, traditional, family-run
businesses are in decline as the younger generation
chooses not to stay in the family firm but to study
or to follow some other occupation. Some choose
to go into a different kind of business. One could
see this social trend as an aspect of globalization.

Bangladeshi businesspeople are eager to build good relationships with their associates and to expand their business horizons, and today there are many foreign companies working successfully in the country. Bangladeshi businesspeople can generally speak and understand English, but they may not understand it as spoken by native English speakers. If you spoke with a strong regional accent, for example, they would find it difficult to understand, and you would have to be patient and speak slowly. When explaining a project, it is usually helpful to show people something on paper.

The Bangladeshi workforce is a mixture of young and middle-aged, skilled and non-skilled people, all of whom are hardworking. Wages differ greatly from one company to another. Workers can read and write a little in Bengali and can sign their names. They are often unionized, and trade unions in big companies can be quite strong. This sometimes creates tensions, but apart from general (that is, political) strikes, the unions are usually careful not to hurt businesses.

The Bangladeshi working week starts on Sunday. Public sector office hours are Sunday to Thursday from 9:00 a.m. to 5:00 p.m., private sector hours between 9:00 a.m. and 6:00 p.m. Private companies have six-day weeks and remain open on Saturdays. On Friday all offices, schools, and colleges are closed. Government offices are closed on Fridays and Saturdays.

BUSINESS CULTURE

There is a hierarchy in business that reflects the wider society. People get respect according to their position. The people subordinate to them not only respect them—they obey them without question and try to please them. This may create some problems, as inefficient people can get away with doing things they should not do.

Bangladesh is very much a relationship-based society, and networking is essential to the conduct of business. Personal recommendation is very important, and time should always be taken to establish trust.

At one time, there used to be a monopoly in many sectors, but not anymore. A free-market economy has brought more enterprising people into the market. There is keen competition among businesses and other organizations such as banks, and the efficiency level has improved a lot because of this.

Business etiquette in Bangladesh is reasonably formal, and proper behavior is expected. Men greet each other with a handshake upon arriving and leaving. Some women also shake hands, but you should wait to see whether they extend their hand first. Otherwise, greet them verbally. Wait until your counterpart moves to a first-name basis before you do the same.

Business cards are exchanged after the initial introduction. Educational qualifications are valued greatly, so be sure to include any university degrees on your card. Always present your business card with your right hand.

MEETINGS

If you want to meet someone, introduce yourself in writing first—e-mail is acceptable—and follow up by phone or e-mail to set the date, time, and venue. Normally the appointment will be made by the personal secretary or assistant to the person you're meeting. Treat her, or him, with respect. Apart from this being good manners, she or he may be a "gatekeeper" who can smooth your path in the future. If you are setting up a meeting with a business group, the process is the same but much more formal.

Punctuality is important. Bangladeshis may be casual about regular meetings, but if the meeting is an important one with a foreign partner or with business associates, they will attend on time. At the meeting you should dress formally: suit and tie for men, and smart and modest (covering the legs) for women.

When you first meet the opposite party, greet them and exchange business cards. The meeting may start with some small talk, but conversation at this stage is formal. Do not forget there is a hierarchical structure in Bangladesh, and observe the niceties. Bengalis may be emotional people, but they leave that outside the meeting room.

Usually the meeting will be led by a senior manager or someone designated by the senior management. The agenda will have been set and written down, but it will not be very rigid. In Bangladesh agendas are only a guideline, so you can relax and feel free to discuss any matters that arise. Meetings can also go on beyond the scheduled time.

PRESENTATIONS

When making a presentation, keep the atmosphere light but serious. Use visual aids like PowerPoint or overhead projectors to help make your case. Your spoken English could be difficult for everyone to understand, but will be clear if accompanied by written material. Keep things brief. Once you have finished, senior people will ask questions and express their views. They generally do not ask the opinion of their juniors. If they did, the junior staff would probably echo support for what they had just said anyway.

NEGOTIATIONS

An aggressive or insistent approach does not go down well with Bangladeshis, who will stay polite throughout the negotiations and try to reach an amicable compromise. They will expect you to go in high and be flexible in bargaining.

The Bangladeshi style is such that you have to read between the lines. They will never say directly, "We can't [won't] do it." They will say, "We will think it over," or "We think it will be difficult," or at best, "We will try."

Decisions may not be made on the spot. If no decision is forthcoming, you may have to meet again and produce more documents. Try to establish who the decision maker is. If your initial meeting has been with middle-ranking managers, then try to gain access to the top management. Remember, if there is more than one decision maker at the top think carefully before talking to them. There may be some underlying tension between them that is not visible to you. If you antagonize any party your deal may not work out. This may take time; if you rush the process, things can go wrong.

CONTRACTS

Commercial practice in Bangladesh is similar to that in the UK. English is commonly used in all business dealings and contracts will be written in English. These are subject to amendment and change at the drafting stage, and you may have to meet the other party several times before you finalize a contract. Remember your relationship with your business partners is very important, and you should try to establish mutual trust before reaching the final stage of signing. Even so, do not rely on verbal undertakings; make sure that everything is written down.

When drawing up a contract Bangladeshi businesspeople will consult legal advisers. Construct the language of your contract carefully and make sure the other party is clear on all clauses. These proceedings take time and patience. A lawyer is usually present at the signing stage.

Contracts are binding in Bangladesh, but can be made flexible by mutual agreement.

MANAGING DISAGREEMENT
If a contract is made in accordance with Bangladesh law, any party can go to court if it is breached. If made under international law, specific mention of the relevant international treaty—for example the Paris Treaty, or the Singapore Treaty—has to be made for the aggrieved party to seek remedy in an international court. In that case, no remedy is available in Bangladesh's national courts. If you do pursue legal action in Bangladesh, the courts are generally efficient and the Supreme Court has a bench to deal expeditiously with commercial disputes.

If problems should arise in an office where you are working with Bangladeshi associates, it is wise to avoid confrontation. The other party may not always express their disagreement openly. They may keep quiet. Remember, confidentiality is very important. Keep your feelings to yourself when things are not going well, then find out what may have gone wrong. If there is a disagreement, talk it over carefully and find a way out. Do not rush to judgment.

CORRUPTION

Undeniably there is corruption in Bangladesh, as there is in any rapidly growing economy. Sometimes transparency in transactions or deals may be lacking. But the corruption is not as universal or widespread as it used to be only a few years ago. Bangladesh has improved its position in Transparency International's global corruption index by one notch. It ranked 27 out of 100 in 2013; in 2012 it was 26.

You may well encounter petty corruption in your day-to-day dealings, but bureaucracy and red tape are much more of a problem when doing business in Bangladesh. If you do not spend a little money, your file may not move at all. A clerk may not respond to your requests, and will only eventually agree to do your paperwork in exchange for some incentive. You have to know how to handle this  problem. Try taking a local person along, one who knows the way these things work, when you go to any office. Sometimes the people at the top of a company turn a blind eye to what is going on under their noses for the sake of harmony, as this is such a deep-rooted social problem.

The giving and receiving of small gifts is common in a business context, as is entertainment. This is completely normal and above board and in no way indicates corrupt practices.

WOMEN IN BUSINESS

Unlike many other countries where Muslims form the majority of the population, in Bangladesh women are active in business, and are working hard for economic and social empowerment. Having overcome family and social barriers, Bangladeshi businesswomen tend to be strong, dedicated, and capable of leadership. Even women from low-income families are starting small businesses with the help of NGOs and loans from the Grameen Bank, the Bangladesh Rural Advancement Committee (BRAC), and other similar agencies. Many NGOs run projects to help village women start their own businesses.

There is a large number of women entrepreneurs in Bangladesh and they are very

organized, with their own associations and chambers of commerce. The Women Entrepreneur Association of Bangladesh (WEAB) was established in 2000 to create a platform for businesswomen in a competitive field dominated by men. It has branches outside Dhaka. WEAB's objective is to develop a support system for women entrepreneurs to improve the quality of their products as well as to meet the constantly changing market demand.

The Bangladesh Women Chamber of Commerce and Industry (BWCCI) was established in 2001 as a non-profit, non-political organization dedicated to encouraging and strengthening women's participation as entrepreneurs in the private sector. It promotes a women-friendly business environment. BWCCI lobbies for women entrepreneurs from the micro to the macro level, to assist their growth and to improve their social and economic prospects. Its members come from the entire range of the socioeconomic spectrum.

The Bangladesh Federation of Women Entrepreneurs (BFWE) was founded in 2006. This is a non-profit organization that offers networking opportunities and a range of benefits to women entrepreneurs. BFWE encourages women to support each other, and promotes the growth of women-owned enterprises through research and the sharing of information.

chapter nine

COMMUNICATING

LANGUAGE

Bangladesh is a monolingual country. The state
language is Bengali (*Bangla*), which is the mother
tongue of the majority of people in Bangladesh.
There are dialects in every district, and the ethnic
minorities have their own languages. Bengali is an

Eastern Indo-Aryan
language shared with the
people of the Indian state
of West Bengal. In terms
of number of speakers
(more than 200 million),
it is the seventh-largest
language in the world.
Bengali is perhaps the
only language to form the

basis on which an independent state was created.

The earliest known example of Bengali literature
is the *Charyapadas*, discovered in Nepal by the
scholar Haraprasad Shastri. These are songs
composed by *siddhacharyas*, teachers of the
tantric Shahajiya sect of Buddhism, who were
mystic poets.

Bengali script is shared, with minor variations,
with Assamese. It is written from left to right and is
characterized by a horizontal line along the top of

the letters. Vowels are written as diacritics attached to the consonants.

Today there are two forms of Bengali—one is *Promita*, or standard, and the other is *Chalita*, or colloquial. The Bengali vocabulary is rich in words borrowed from other languages, such as English and Persian (and through Persian some Arabic and Turkish). In Bangladesh most official work within the country is done in Bengali, but English is used in diplomacy, trade, and higher education and research. Some people speak in dialect at home, but will generally use *Promita*, or standard Bengali, for academic and literary purposes. When they speak to people outside their homes, they speak standard Bengali.

In the capital, Dhaka, and other major cities, many people can speak English. They may not be very articulate, but you can communicate with them. Government, NGO, and other officials can speak English. In the resorts, staff can speak a little English as they frequently have foreign guests.

GREETINGS

When greeting or addressing someone in this traditional society, you have to remember a few things: relationship, religion, and age. You must show respect to elders. Hugging or kissing is not done. You can shake hands with Bangladeshi men, but be careful about physical contact with women. If they extend their hand, you can shake it. Otherwise greet them only with a smile or a nod. You can say "*Assalamo alaikum*" if she is a Muslim, or "*Namaskar*" if she is Hindu; or you can just say "Hello," which is universal in this modern age.

SOME BENGALI PHRASES

People will be delighted if you make the effort to learn some Bengali phrases. Here are a few for starters:

Aapnar naam ki? What is your name?

Aami ekhane notun. I am new here.

Aapni kemon achhen? How are you?

Aami bhalo achhi. I am fine.

Ki obosthha? What's up?

Ek cup cha. A cup of tea.

Onugroho kore ek glass pani din.
Please give me a glass of water.

Aapni ei jaigata chenen? Do you know this place?

Shekhane kibhabe jabo? How can I go there?

Bharah koto? What's the fare?

Kota baje? What is the time?

Kichhu kenakata kora dorkar. Need to do some shopping.

Daam koto? What's the price?

Aamar jabar somoy hoye gechhe. It's time for me to go.

Aabar dekha hobey. See you again.

BODY LANGUAGE

Bangladeshis are physically very expressive and use a lot of gestures while talking. As you may face language problems, some non-verbal communication by gesture on your part may be needed. Your body language is important as it shows whether you are paying respect or not. Here are some dos and don'ts.

- Do not put your feet up; do not slouch; do not sit with your back to someone.
- Whistling or pointing your finger at someone is rude.
- You can call the waiter in a restaurant by tapping a spoon on the plates, glasses, or cups. You can also wave.
- When someone is talking, you must listen attentively. If your interlocutor is an elderly or respected person, try not to maintain eye contact for too long. Glancing at them from time to time is OK.
- In Bangladesh, a nod means "yes" and shaking the head sideways means "no."
- You must give personal space to the person you are talking to. Do not sit very close to people unless they are very close friends, especially if they are women.

HUMOR

All Bengalis have a keen sense of humor. There is a saying: "*Eto bhongo Bongodesh, tobu rongo bhora*" ("Bengal is so much broken, yet full of humor"). They will joke about almost anything, from relationships to politics, which is a favorite topic. Sometimes these jokes can be very crude or cruel, and if someone close to you tells you such a joke do not repeat it in front of others as Bangladeshis are very politically divided. All Bengalis enjoy slapstick comedy, but they also like puns and wordplay. Bengalis have long been regarded as the intellectuals of the subcontinent.

Frankly Speaking
"I got a divorce from my husband because of religion."
"How come?"
"My husband thinks he is God, but I don't."

Humor features largely in films, theater, and songs. Bangladeshi blockbuster films tend to include comedic interludes to provide light relief, which sometimes can be a little vulgar.

THE MEDIA
The communications sector in Bangladesh has changed dramatically in recent years. Incentives from both the government and the private sector have helped it grow and it is now a major part of the economy. Because it is such a populous country, Bangladesh is a huge market that has attracted many foreigners to invest in this sector.

Press
The country has a long tradition of journalism. Newspapers and periodicals were first published in Bengal in the last quarter of the eighteenth century. The first English weekly came out from Dhaka in 1856. Edited by A. R. Forbes, it was called the *Dhaka News*.

After the fall of General Ershad in 1990, the press in Bangladesh gradually regained its independence. Today it is vibrant and free and there is a plethora of newspapers and periodicals, reflecting a broad spectrum of opinion. Most of the papers are serious broadsheets. There are popular tabloids, too, but most of these are local publications in district towns. There are women's magazines and specialist magazines for film, sports, trade and commerce, and literature. The majority of these publications are in Bengali, but there are a few very good English daily newspapers and magazines as well.

International and national news agencies are important sources of information. The Bangladesh Press Institute promotes good journalism, provides in-service training for working journalists, and helps them in their research work. The Bangladesh Press Council was established to preserve the freedom of the press and to improve the standard of newspapers and news agencies in Bangladesh.

The main quality Bengali newspapers are *Ittefaq*, *Songbad*, *Prothom Alo*, *Kaler Kantha*, *Janakantha*, *Jugantor*, and *Shomokal*. The main English-language newspapers are the *Daily Star*, *The Independent*, *New Age*, *Daily Sun*, *Bangladesh Observer*, and *The New Nation*.

The Bengali financial papers include *Amader Orthoneeti*, *Banikbarta*, and, in English, the *Financial Express*. Most of the dailies and weeklies now have online editions. Also there are dedicated online news media.

New newspapers come out from time to time even though the newspaper readership is not very large. It is high in urban areas and very low in rural areas. But the hunger for news is undoubtedly there. Sometimes, in a rural marketplace, one

person will read the newspaper aloud as others
eagerly listen.

Television

The first television
transmission was a pilot project
in Dhaka on December 25, 1964,
using a 300-watt transmitter with a
radius of just under 10 miles (16
km). The television corporation was
nationalized after Independence in 1972.
Today there are many private television channels
broadcasting in Bengali. Audiences in Bangladesh
can also receive most of the Indian channels,
BBC World, CNN, and many others.

Besides the government-owned BTV and BTV
World there are twenty-seven private TV channels
including a few 24-hour news channels. New
channels emerge from time to time.

Radio

Radio in the eastern part of Bengal started in Dhaka
on December 16, 1939. The first radio station was
called *Dhaka Dhawani Bistar Kendra* (Dhaka
Sound Broadcasting Station) and had a 5-kilowatt
medium-wave transmitter. After partition in 1947,
Dhaka radio continued its transmission under a
new name, Radio Pakistan Dhaka.

Radio transmission closely reflected the political
turmoil of this region. In 1952, during the
Language Movement, the whole staff of Dhaka
Radio boycotted it in protest at the killing of the
martyrs. On March 7, 1971, the staff closed down
transmission and left the station after the Pakistan
government made the decision not to broadcast the

historic speech of Sheikh Mujibur Rahman.
Normal transmission began the next day, when
the Pakistan military authority agreed to put the
historic speech on the air. After midnight on
March 25, 1971, when the Pakistan armed forces
started the campaign of genocide in Dhaka, the
declaration of independence on behalf of the
charismatic Mujibur Rahman was broadcast the
next day from Chittagong station, which termed
itself the *Swadhin Bangla Biplobi Betar
Kendra* (Revolutionary Radio Center of
Independent Bengal). Later, during the nine-
month liberation war, a radio station called
Swadhin Bangla Betar Kendra (Radio Center of
Independent Bengal) transmitted news and other
inspiring programs from across the border. After
independence, the radio stations in Bangladesh
merged into a single national radio network.

In 2008, the Ministry of Information announced
the Community Radio Installation, Broadcast and
Operation Policy, which established sixteen
community radio stations. To ensure
the free flow of information to the
people, the government enacted the
Right to Information Act 2009.
Community radio stations are a
strong step toward empowering rural
people. There are many FM radio
broadcasters in Bangladesh, catering mainly to the
younger generation. You can also listen to FM
radio online. The BBC FM service is also available.

The BBC World Service, including the language
services, the Voice of America (VOA), Radio
Beijing, All-India Radio, Deutsche Welle, and other
foreign radio services are all available. There is no

restriction on listening to any radio. The BBC
World Service is very popular in Bangladesh, as is
the VOA.

SERVICES
Telecommunications
After independence in 1971, the Bangladesh
Telephone and Telegraph Board was created as part
of the Ministry of Posts and Telecommunications
to run the services on a commercial basis. The
Board controls all telecommunications in the
country. The state-owned telecommunications
system operates in all urban areas; there are no
landline services in rural areas. However, private
entrepreneurs provide cell phone and e-mail
services, and there are many cell phone operators.
The Bangladesh Rural Telecom Authority was, in
1989, the first private company to get a license
from the government to operate and
maintain digital phone exchanges in
200 *upazilas* (subdistricts).

Cell phone prices range from
1,000 Taka (US $12.89) to
70,000 Taka (US $902.18).
SIM cards cost about 60 to
70 Taka (US $ 0.77 to US $0.90). To buy them you
need some basic documentation such as your
passport and a passport-sized photograph. Unlike
many other countries, in Bangladesh once you buy
a SIM card it lasts forever. All you need to do is

maintain a certain number of minutes.
Mobile phone calls are cheap. Rates
differ, but average 1.92 Taka (US $0.02)
per minute.

To call Bangladesh from another country you need to dial 00-88 + the city code (Dhaka is 02, Chittagong 031, Khulna 041, Sylhet 0821, Rajshahi 0721), then the telephone number.

Internet

Internet access in Bangladesh is widely available in the cities. There are Internet cafés in the big cities and in many small towns, particularly where the government has established information centers, even at *upazila* level. Some hotels also offer Internet access. Satellite Internet in Bangladesh enables people to access the Internet where there is no terrestrial connection. Sometimes the speed may not be very fast, but the cost is quite low.

The social impact of the Internet has been overwhelming in several respects. Personal connections are now maintained mainly through the Internet. In the educational sector, people use it extensively to download materials and to share and exchange ideas; and in the medical sector people use telemedicine facilities a lot. Facebook and blogging are common among the young, and not totally unknown to the older generation. The recent Shabagh Movement was initiated by a handful of bloggers; thousands of people responded, and it became history.

E-commerce (*kena-becha*) is no longer unfamiliar to businesspeople, big or small, rural or urban. E-banking is very popular and is increasing. In 2013, the number of Internet users in Bangladesh increased to 33 million.

Rural culture in Bangladesh is undergoing a profound change as a result of the introduction of the Internet and cell phones. This is not necessarily negative or harmful. Farmers, fisher folk, and businesspeople use mobile and Internet facilities for business, and to settle matters such as supply, price, and so on.

The main service providers are BTCL (Bangladesh Telecommunications Company Limited), Citech, Cybernet BRAC, DRIK, PROSHIKA, and all the telephone companies, namely Banglalink, Grameen, Robi, and Airtel.

Bangladesh's Internet country code is ".bd".

Mail

The postal service in Bangladesh is reliable, quick, and reasonably priced. The Post Office is still run by a government department. It provides the community with a variety of services: mailing letters, handling parcels, tracking and tracing, courier delivery, foreign money orders, E-Post (electronic mail service), financial services, postboxes, and more. Airmail to Europe takes between three and four days. The number of post offices in urban areas has declined in recent years as most people now use e-mail, but you can still find post offices in rural areas where people use them not only to send letters and packages, but also for services such as money transfer.

Courier services are popular. Apart from international companies such as DHL and FedEx, there are Continental Courier Service, Excelsior Express, Sundarban Courier Service, Air Express Services, and others. Most of the intercity transport companies also run courier services.

These services are speedy and reliable, and if you want to send something within the country, they are quite cheap.

CONCLUSION

Bangladesh is geopolitically important in the region as the bridge between South and Southeast Asia. It shares borders, and sometimes cultures, with northeastern Indian states that are politically sensitive for India. It is not an affluent country, and is frequently hit by natural disasters, but its human capital is remarkable. The spirit of enterprise among the young is reflected in its economy, and the pioneering microfinance policies of the Grameen Bank have created an innovative way of enabling people to lift themselves out of poverty that has become a model for the world.

Bangladesh has a unique and fascinating cultural heritage, much of which it shares with West Bengal. Its distinctive form of Islam is tolerant, open, and inclusive, and its social life is a mix of the modern and traditional. For a crowded, hot, and humid country, the people are very easygoing and relaxed. When you first arrive, you may find the crush of humanity, the traffic chaos, and the intrusive curiosity of the small crowd that seems to follow you around overwhelming. This inquisitiveness is wholly benevolent and reflects a genuine desire to know more about you and your culture. Bangladeshis are friendly and hospitable. They are also politically passionate, and very polarized today, so visitors should avoid political discussions and give rallies and demonstrations a wide berth.

The more you get to know and understand the Bangladeshis, the more you'll like them. They are extraordinarily resilient. Accustomed to coping with disasters, both natural and man made, they'll put aside their differences to cooperate when faced with a crisis. You will discover a warm and generous people who welcome you with unaffected sincerity and hospitality. It is often said that you may come to Bangladesh as a stranger, but you'll leave as a friend.

Further Reading

Bass, Gary. J. *The Blood Telegram: India's Secret War in East Pakistan*. New York: Random House, 2013.

Guhathakurta, Meghna and Willem van Schendel. *The Bangladesh Reader: History, Culture, Politics*. Durham, North Carolina: Duke University Press, 2013.

Mamoon, Muntasir. *Nineteenth-Century East Bengal*. Dhaka: University Press Limited, 2010.

Rahman, A.T. Rafiqur. *Bangladesh in the Mirror: An Outsider Perspective on a Struggling Democracy*. Dhaka: University Press Limited, 2006.

Rahman, Sheikh Mujibur. *The Unfinished Memoir*. Transl. Fakrul Alam. Dhaka: University Press Limited, 2012.

Schendel, Willem van. *A History of Bangladesh*. Cambridge: Cambridge University Press, 2009.

Sengupta, Nitish. *Land of Two Rivers*. New Delhi: Penguin Books India, 2011.

Yunus, Muhammad. *Building Social Business: The New Kind of Capitalism that Serves Humanity's Most Pressing Needs*. Dhaka: University Press Limited, 2010.

culture smart! bangladesh

Index

168

culture smart! bangladesh

Acknowledgments

Many thanks for all their help to my friends Sultana Kamal, Abdul Mannan, Mobashera Khanam, Mofidul Haque, Muntasir Mamoon, Abul Mansur; to my brother-in-law Didar Hosain, my sister Shoma Rahman, and my life partner Sagar Chaudhury. Thank you, Nick Nugent and Daniel Nelson, for remembering me, and Geoffrey, for your patience.